Lovers' Guide

Lovers' Guide to

PALMISTRY

Mary E. Anderson

JAVELIN BOOKS
POOLE · NEW YORK · SYDNEY

First published in the UK 1986 by Javelin Books,
Link House, West Street, Poole, Dorset, BH15 1LL.

Distributed in the United States by
Sterling Publishing Co., Inc.,
2 Park Avenue, New York, NY 10016

Distributed in Australia by
Capricorn Link (Australia) Pty Ltd.,
PO Box 665, Lane Cove, NSW 2066

British Library Cataloguing in Publication Data

Anderson, Mary E.
  The lovers' guide to palmistry.
  1. Palmistry and sex
  I. Title
  133.6   BF935.S4

ISBN 0 7137 1711 4

Typesetting by Poole Typesetting (Wessex) Ltd.
Reproduced, printed and bound in Great Britain by
Hazell Watson & Viney Limited,
Member of the BPCC Group,
Aylesbury, Bucks

To Dickie who never lived to see the end of this book.

My gratitude and thanks to Bill Atkinson, Johan Hjelmborg, Andrew Fitzherbert and other members of the Society for the Study of Physiological Patterns who taught me all I know about Palmistry, and to my friends Henri and Jilly without whose valuable help this book would never have seen the light of day.

If you are interested in becoming a member of the above Society, then write to The Hon. Secretary, S.S.P.P., 39 Larchwood House, Baywood Square, Chigwell, Essex, UK.

Contents

Introduction

Few people realise that they are carrying around a full-scale map of their character and potentialities. Like any other map the reader needs to understand the signs, but the amateur hand analyst can derive a lot of pleasure, profit, and information from understanding the basic simplicity of the art.

It is clearly true that man or woman is a social animal; we are not constructed to live alone, to make progress through life as loners. It is through our relationship experiences that we grow, develop, and mature; we literally have the clue to self-understanding in our own hands.

Hand analysis can help in: vocational guidance; partnership assessment, as it will be shown in this work; psychological diagnosis; and with certain medical problems. To date it seems to have suffered due to its association with seaside fortune-telling, but of course it is more than this. A doctor has written a book telling of his use of hand prints in his practice, in which he highlights the signs of health failure as seen in the hands. Another doctor studied the hand prints of disturbed children and young adults. In the last 50 years orthodox professional bodies such as psychologists, psychiatrists and others involved in medicine and counselling are seriously studying hands and skin patterns.

Hopefully we will now be travelling on a road which will lead to the use of handreading on an even wider scale both for interest and information, and this will contribute to the growth in human awareness which is part of the blessing of the coming Aquarian Age.

Palmistry is a fascinating study, and there is and has been in existence for some fifty years a Society for the Study of Physiological Patterns for the study and research of hand outlines, prints and patterns, which is also a teaching faculty.

When you come to think of it, marriage is probably the most important step you are going to take in your whole life; and so many marriages are undertaken for the wrong motives, or simply for superficial reasons, such as the very handsome profile of the loved one, which after all is not going to add one iota to the quality and depth of the relationship. Therefore, anything which helps someone in love to understand himself and his partner better can be invaluable. The same interest would, I think, be generated by family members, by friends and by associates or partners in a business sense.

You do not need to be a genius to gain a good working knowledge of Palmistry. Those important things that you want to know about a new lover and about yourself as a lover or mate really are to be found in the hand. First of all is he/she sincere? Then, is he/she kind, generous, mean, the faithful type or the philanderer? All these questions and many more can be answered by correct interpretation of the hands. With this knowledge there is really no need to go in 'blind' to a permanent relationship, or a marriage. Palmistry can be the map which you can learn to read to help you understand yourself, your attitudes, needs, limitations and your relationships, and so to improve these if necessary.

It is said that it is love which makes the world go round, and so perhaps it is the lack of fulfilling relationships which makes the world's progress so unnerving for many humans. Everything is polarity – our consciousness obeys this law, and without it nothing could exist; obvious examples are good and evil, light and dark, man and woman. These appear to us as contrasting factors, but in reality each needs the other for existence; so, as the old song goes from the film *Casablanca*, *'man needs woman and woman needs man'*, and the way to happiness for most of us is through satisfying emotional and romantic relationships.

So that we do not become too exclusive and build up tremendously satisfying twosomes, we should also widen our horizons to include compatible friendships, which provide us with good reliable background support socially; so that, should the partnership be broken up for any reason, the partner left by this change is still enclosed within a comfortable circle of understanding friends. This is very important now as I have found in my practice, for families are less closely-knit, and movement and early independence of children and other family members has meant that families, which were the main support of any isolated member, just do not exist. This role has been taken over by our friends, so it behoves us to choose these wisely, for they may have to be our mainstay in the case of trouble.

Likewise, of course, choice of partner is all-important, as we have already mentioned, for relationships can bring joy or grief and so shape our lives for growth and progress if they are fulfilling.

A little careful study of this book then can reveal a lover's or friend's emotional potential, their way of thinking, their hidden depths and above all their compatibility. It can point out many things which are helpful to successful sharing and understanding. Have we perhaps some emotional blocks which prevent us being as successful in our relationships as we might be? Palmistry can answer this both for ourselves and also in reference to our loved ones.

Throughout this book I have written for an imaginary couple who are willing to look at the indications in their hands together and even to make notes on their findings. Happily they have a small table between them and sitting opposite one another are able to view each other's hands in turn. If the progress of our two friends is not specifically commented on in every chapter, they are still considered to be there as being essential to the purpose of the book, which is to be a guide to prospective friends and lovers as well as helping you to understand members of your family.

We really start on a more concentrated note in Chapter 3 where we formally usher in our friends.

1 The Man's Viewpoint

Let's enjoy an intuitive, observant trip trying to assess a lover, friend, or prospective partner, taking it first of all from the man's viewpoint.

'Never marry a woman with a square hand or she'll rule your life', is a quotation from the great Palmist, Comte de St. Germain, who wrote his greatest work *Palmistry For Professional Purposes* in 1897.

If picking a partner by the hand shape was important then, it is still important now. As society becomes more complex, so do the people who live in it. For instance, a girl with a square palm today is far more of an asset from the point of view of being practical, hard-working and able to manage, because women today will not stand for being just a decoration, and most women work anyway. Therefore, unless you have pots of money, marry a girl with square hands.

As we will point out later in more detail, a study of the hand shape is essential when choosing a partner. The advantage of knowing your hand shapes means that you can read across the room at a party, when being introduced (the handshake is important), and when the other person isn't looking.

There is an intuitive aspect to hand-reading, which you can learn in five minutes, and which is very good for quick personality assessments.

If you see hands that are thin, drooping and pale, lacking in expression, then you have a withdrawn, quiet personality that is rather passive and lacking in energy. Remember, this type need a lot of support and attention and if you have the time and a very caring nature, this one is for you, perhaps.

This system is accurate even though it is intuitive, because this is based on the first impression of the hand. After comparing a few hands you will see that there is as much expression shown in the hands as there is in the face; in fact more so, for, while people may control their expressions or put on an act, the movement of their hands always gives them away.

You don't have to be a genius to spot the nervous edgy types whose fingers are always on the move, or the emotional Latin lovers who speak with their hands and often move them about quite dangerously.

The full, plump, pink hands, with fine skin, pink colour, graceful fingers, belong to the real beauties of the world, the sort that model nail varnish. These girls don't mind being decorative, but tend to organise other people quite readily. And although they are quite happy being show-pieces (essentially for a career man) they can turn out to be quite expensive. If the hands are perfect they can be unbelievably lazy. I did say they like organising other people, often on the basis of 'darling bring me that' or 'would you please pass me this'.

If this isn't enough and you are still keen on perfection, first remember that this lady is not half as soft as she makes herself out to be and can react quite forcibly when need be, especially so if the hand has any real firmness to it and the fingers are long.

If you like a little temper in a girl and enormous energy, look for fingernails that don't seem to reach the end of the finger and where the flesh at the tip of the finger looks quite prominent. It gives the fingers a squared look and the tip has a slightly snub-nosed look. With this girl keep only cheap crockery in the house as it may need frequent replacement. This partner is not all bad, it is simply that the emotions are strong and earthy, and they can be just as affectionate as offensive. With a masculine sort of hand they will be hard-working, show their emotions easily and freely, but be extremely protective.

Thumbs play an important part in judging a prospective partner, lover, friend. Small thumbs on a small hand are not desirable as they indicate a person who is easily led and quite often lacks control. A very long thumb will show that a person is too dominating and in full control of their lives and, therefore, will only be persuaded when they want to be.

If the tip of the thumb is fine, you have someone you can impress. Flatter them to your heart's content and they will love every minute. They realise it's all 'flannel' and soft soap, but nevertheless they like it.

A square tip on the thumb shows that this time it won't work, and here flattery gets you nowhere. Unless they take a liking to you in the first place the only way round this person is with sincerity. They are not the sort you can hurry, either, so be patient and let nature take its course.

If the thumbs are stiff, some formality would be required, and if you make a mistake it may be the only one you will get the chance to make. Not so if the thumb is supple and bends back at the first joint. If the thumb bends back at the tip they are easy-going, tend to make the rules as they go along, and are talkative, sociable creatures.

They will tend to forgive and forget quite often, but never push your luck with these types because they have a nasty way of getting back at you while you are still thinking of apologising. They are, however, friendly creatures at heart, and if you are an unconventional type yourself these are the partners for you as they can adapt.

On the subject of flexibility, flexibility of the hand (back-bending joints) is essential, and with a soft hand even better. If all the fingers bend back from the palm together, when pushed of course, these people can make a home anywhere and will fit into almost any environment. If you are a family type and like everything just so, whether you live in a palace or a pig sty, this type will fall in with your ideas and adapt entirely to your way of life.

Back to the thumbs. The long thin thumb is a studious type, and she will be quite happy with a quiet life, curling up with a good book, and she'll do a lot for peace and quiet.

But if the first joint is thick and knotty you have someone who is quiet on the surface but underneath quite stubborn, and they can usually see right through you. In fact, while she is gazing into your eyes, she is quietly taking you apart and putting you back together again. If the fingers are knotty at the joints as well, it is not imagination, it's really happening . . ..

Be careful with the girl who holds her thumb close to the palm when the hand is relaxed; you won't find it easy to get through to her, but, when you do so, you might be very surprised at what you find. This sort is more prepared to take than to give, not marked for their generosity. They also hold onto secrets and confidences well.

If the thumb bends right out from the hand so that it goes at right angles to the wrist, these are generous, outgoing, open people, and cannot keep anything to themselves, especially if the tip too bends back. These are the real chatterboxes, and if you're the sort who doesn't talk much, keep away from parties because you're shy and can't think of anything to say, bring along this one if you can catch her and she'll open you out quicker than a psychoanalyst. An instant cure for loneliness or depression.

Next to the thumb there is a large pad of flesh with a line round it from the middle of the wrist (Life line). This pad is called the mount of Venus (see Figure 1) and it tells you a lot. For instance, if you want to know if your partner or friend has a lot of energy, look for a large pad under the thumb. To discover if your partner is really sympathetic with her emotions, again look for a large pad.

Do you like travel? If so, you need a partner who also likes travel. If the beginning of the Life line takes a good share of the wrist – half or more, then you're on. If the Life line is so tight into the wrist that the pad is small and the line tucks under itself towards the thumb, there is not such a good resilience in the constitution for overcoming illness; this marks out the homelover who'll only travel from necessity, or possibly even an agoraphobic. So a good pad of Venus that takes up a large portion of the palm with a clear line round it is dynamic, outgoing and purposeful.

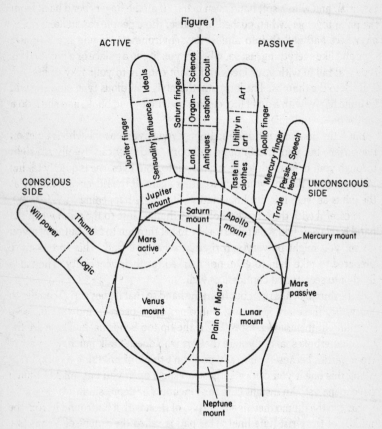

Figure 1

A small thumb here would emphasise the desire for physical outdoor activities – not to mention some of the indoor ones. With the long thumb, of course, such a person would be hard to keep up with and may take the lead more often than you would like.

If the mount of Venus is flat, baggy or stringy-looking, there isn't much energy at all and this is reflected in the amount of warmth and sympathy they show; therefore they need a lot, and the only way to hold such a partner is to give it. If, however, you like a lot of sympathy and affection yourself this is not the one for you.

Have you noticed how like goes to like? We are drawn to those who share our background, ideas and sympathies. Artistic types tend to link with artistic types. Basically here we are talking about people who possess active imaginations and often high anxiety levels. It's useless being married or closely connected with someone who laughs at your worries and fears and preferable to have someone who understands.

So let's have a look at the pad of flesh at the other side of the palm opposite the mount of Venus. This side of the hand, under the little finger, is known as the percussion, because it's the bit we bang the table with or drum, because it's a percussion instrument.

Now, if we look at the wrist where the palm begins, we have the mount of Venus on one side and the mount of Luna on the other, the percussion side (see Figure 1). Some palms are so prominent that they appear as a step up from the wrist.

If you hold your hand up in front of you, you can see if both mounts are level at the base. If the base of the palm is level, this is fine, your responses are good and well balanced. If the mount of Luna is slightly higher than the mount of Venus then you need a lot more stimulus in your life than the average person and may find it in driving fast, gambling or hard liquor.

If the mount of Luna drops down into the wrist and is lower than the mount of Venus you have a terrific imagination, will anticipate danger, may even be frightened of the dark or what's around the corner. In any case you need less stimulus in your life as your anxiety level will be a little higher than normal. This excess of imagination can be turned into poetry with lots of feeling, if the hand is long and narrow.

If the side of the hand curves out (bulges) there is much originality and a desire to create, whereas if the edge of the hand is straight, interpretation of other people's ideas is the real talent, such as music, language, and communication generally.

If you are looking for a girl with a strong personality, it's a good idea to look for a forceful first finger – one that looks a bit longer than the third finger, as this is the finger people poke you in the ribs with from time to time. You can see how this would indicate the type of personality! These people are often clever and most certainly sure of themselves and know what they are good at. Their organising ability is good, so that if you are a slow thinker they can make up your mind for you double quick.

How serious is your partner going to be? The finger of Saturn (the middle one) gives you some indication of this. If it looks very long compared to the other fingers, then you may well have a very moody type on your hands and one who takes a very serious attitude to life. Of course there are advantages, they will be careful with money, plan ahead and build for the future; but be careful if the fingers are thick – they may even become miserly and end up with lots in the bank and holes in your socks. But, generally speaking, these people are very cautious and if you are the sort of chap that can't manage money at all and don't go out too often, this one is for you.

Of course, if you do like to go out and play free and easy with your hard-earned cash, then pick a girl with a short Saturn (middle finger). They can be quite frivolous and do well at parties and can make a lot of small talk, because to them nothing has tremendous importance. They never seem to be short of a few bob as they always know where to get it. As a matter of interest, people whose middle finger was as long as the Apollo (third finger) were considered to be extremely good pickpockets and still are, as the art of dipping depends on the scissor action of these two fingers sliding into people's pockets and gently coaxing out the wallet. These fingers being of equal length was always an asset for this particular profession. So if this happy-go-lucky type is for you, keep an eye out for a short Saturn.

The ring finger is in its own way a very important finger to look at in relation to character – after all this is the finger you will eventually put the ring on, so it is worth finding out now what the finger is like before you start decorating it. Does she already wear a ring on this finger? On the right hand it is a sign of availability, because the right hand is the outgoing side of the personality. The left hand, of course, is more meaningful as it demonstrates one's inner feelings and private life. A ring on this finger, for instance, apart from meaning she's already engaged, may simply be an indication that there are partners available when she is ready and she is well aware of this.

A long Apollo (third finger) is a good indication of emotional response. These people tend to take a chance and stick their necks out from time to time out of curiosity to see what will happen, or just for the hell of it. There is a more adventurous go-ahead spirit in such a girl than you can imagine.

If the ring finger stands away from the middle finger, so that there is a wide gap when the hands are at rest, they are genuinely way out! The old-fashioned term is bohemian. They refuse to dress like drop-outs to show that they are drop-outs, because this is only another way of conforming. They are drop-outs pure and simple, and if other people are doing it they do something else. So if you are looking for the unpredictable, try this one.

If the Apollo (third finger) lies close to the middle finger you have a partner who is co-operative, because she doesn't like doing things on her own and her life will not be lived for kicks. To be emotionally satisfied she needs a partner she feels is worthwhile. These people are loyal and reliable.

The Mercury (fourth finger) is a very peculiar finger – it is the little one that sits on the edge of the hand and seems to mind its own business.

The side of the hand indicates the unconscious nature, just as the mount of Luna shows the imagination, our instincts and fears, so the little finger shows our unconscious activities. To some degree it is a good indication of sex drive, of a talent for persuasiveness; and it is not surprising the finger is important when we consider that Oriental culture allows the little fingernails to grow extremely long to mark out the gentleman who doesn't have to work for a living. From the Victorian times, the little finger was stuck up in the air during the process of tea drinking – it was considered that women who did this were putting on airs and graces when really they were demonstrating their independence.

The little finger that curls itself under the others is a mark of prudishness; spaced too far away from the others it shows independence of action, a partner who does not want to be tied to home, or some say a family rift exists. A sharp tip indicates sarcasm. A long finger shows the ability to manipulate other people. If crooked, they have the ability to be dishonest.

But what you really want to know is – is your partner sexy? And this is indicated quite clearly by a long finger with a fine tip, a knotty second joint and a plump third joint, next to the palm.

Incidentally, at the second joint of this finger there is often an inward bend towards the palm and the joint is locked and cannot be straightened. Such a pronounced kink in the finger often indicates a woman who has painful periods and difficulty in childbirth.

2 The Woman's Viewpoint

Choosing a mate for a woman can be a serious business. In fact little girls' ambitions seem to arrange themselves around the sort of husband they will choose; perhaps women's lib will change all this. Consequently, the sort of social class they will have, the house, the country they will live in and so on is the subject of early fantasies and dreams, quite apart from the chap they will eventually marry.

It is more important for a girl to make the right choice than it is for a man, because for a woman the change can be very dramatic and total, even to a change of name (an interesting point for numerologists). A woman tends to be the driving force behind a man; if she is ambitious she will spur him on to bigger and better things. If she likes him cuddly she will feed him up, and if she wants him to last a long time she'll make sure he's relaxed and content. But choosing the raw material at first is as important as what happens afterwards. So let's look at a few examples.

First glance at a man's hands will show whether he digs ditches or works in an office, or doesn't have to work at all. We are back to our intuitive hand-reading, you'll notice. If a man's hands are large, coarse in texture, you have a hard worker on your hands. If the thumbs are long, he can run his own business, so there need be no shortage of cash.

If the fingers are heavy and square at the tips your partner will be pedantic, orthodox, will have a love of order, perhaps even discipline. He is not a 'get rich quick' merchant, but he is protective, plans for the future, and has all the old-fashioned qualities that may be dull, but make for a stable and lasting marriage. If you are interested in this type, first be sure he has a decent Fate line (see Fig. 2). By 'decent', I mean clear and well-formed.

If the thumb is on the short side, and perhaps the fingers too, he will be even more in favour of physical activity, but less inclined to plan ahead, so you will find you have to manage the cash matters. If the thumb is on the weak side, do be sure you get your hands on the cash first, because if the

Figure 2

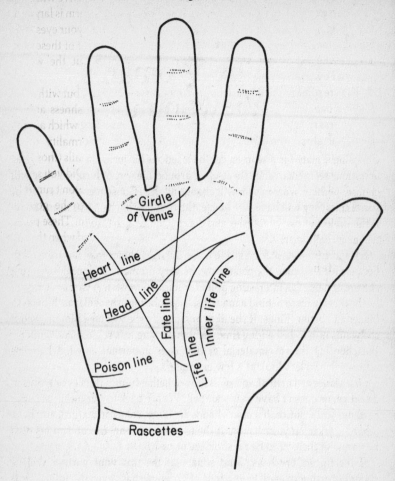

second phalange (joint) of the thumb has a waist and the finger tips aren't heavy squares, you might find your impetuous old devil of a husband has got through the lot on the way home. At least life won't be dull!

Back to intuitive hand-reading. If this large, coarse, masculine hand is on the stiff side with the fingers tending to curl in and the thumbs always held close to the hand, give him a miss as he's likely to be very tight-fisted. You can often tell, because they don't talk much either. These people can be tight with everything. These strong, silent types can be very attractive with their air of mystery, but as they don't come across much, their charm is largely in your imagination. So forget the features for a moment, drag your eyes away from the face and get back to the hands. There are quite a lot of these types about, who for some strange reason attract women, but the women attracted by these types often have a rude awakening.

Here are some of the things I mean. A nice smile is all right, but with a cold clammy handshake it's not for you. Coldness equals selfishness and the clamminess may be some physical disorder. In fact, anything which appears abnormal about the hand may simply reflect the abnormality of the personality. For instance, it is natural to have moons on the nails (those little blue semi-circles at the palm end of the nail are the moons). Did you say the boyfriend hasn't got any? A sure sign he's not domesticated. Don't run away with the idea that you'll change all that. Because when he goes on walkabouts, you might find there's the soul of a gipsy in him. These people may well marry, but it's often later than the average male, and when they are married home can be a convenience rather than a home.

They are fine as salesmen, representatives and so on, but if you don't want a husband travelling in ladies' underwear, keep away.

What you should look for in a hand basically is what you look for in the rest of the man – good proportions. A little practice looking at people standing in bus queues and on the underground will train your eyes as to what the ideal looks like.

You want a hand neither too fat nor too thin (the former is sensual, the latter ascetic), but padded with solid flesh and neither too hard nor too soft to touch.

If you are a career girl who works with her head rather than her hands, the leaner sort of hands might appeal to you in a partner. Just as the ideal for a physical type of girl would be the more physical hands in a man so the personal ideals you are looking for require you to shop around a little and see what you like.

Your man should be able to express himself emotionally; if the stiff ones can't, then it stands to reason the supple ones can. Hence the reputation of the Latin lovers who virtually talk with their hands and can't say much if their hands are stuck in their pockets.

If the hands are tiny with fine skin, slim fingers, pointed thumbs, he may sweep you off your feet. He's got more chat than you'd ever believe possible. Too much in fact, and there's no need to believe any of it, because these people are all talk and no do.

If they are small in stature with dark hair, they are the super salesmen of this world, and with a long well-formed little finger, that's the one they'll twist you round, they will tell you anything you want to know and they have so much skill; flattery gets them everywhere.

Girls tend to fall in love with their doctors. You can learn a lot from looking at your doctor's hands. Usually they are a good size, very capable-looking, heavy fingers, long, with well-formed nails. That is the sort to look for.

A long Mercury (little finger) on these hands shows cleverness, skill, sexual prowess, a good sense of value for money and all sorts of natural talents.

If the little finger is too thin, your man is too ascetic, it has to be the right time and place. If the little finger is too podgy, especially with a ring, this man likes his pleasures too much, he is indolent and often selfish.

If you like the sporting type, hair on the back of the hands isn't necessary, but it's a start because it confirms that your man is a sporting type and definitely an 'out of doors' character, especially with a large mount of Venus. Sometimes the hair is only on the back of the hand behind the little finger. It's quite difficult to get these types out of the bedroom. If the hair is on the right hand behind the little finger, try waving a fiver under their nose; it usually stirs their enthusiasm. The little finger is also a good indicator of a man's ability to communicate with others.

The left hand being the more intimate side of life and the right hand his business activities, a ring on the little finger gives him away every time.

You may like a man who has more refinement and *savoir faire*. If so, you need a hand which is not so broad and therefore less materialistic, a hand that looks longish because of this, but with square tips to the fingers, a fine skin texture, but a good colour; not the pale wishy-washy lifeless-looking hand of the man who does nothing unless he has to do it. You want to see a good healthy pink that glows with vitality, and a good firmness to the grip. You expect the fingers to be slimmer and of course the thumb, but these digits should not be too thin, bony-looking and dried out. They should be expressive in their mobility, but without the agitation of our Latin lover types.

If the skin is so fine at the back of the hand that the veins can be seen, and these stand up slightly on the back of the hand, then you have an academic quality, refinement plus maturity. The fingernails in this case should be slightly oblong, otherwise the emotional depths may be lacking. If there is over-refinement and boniness to these hands, then you have the old-fashioned aristocrat – the snappy dresser who is over-particular about his food, hygiene, and so on and so forth. They can be too finicky for words. Unless you are finicky too, don't bother. They can make your life a misery.

While we are on the subject of fingernails, it is worth noting that a long narrow nail that comes to a point at the palm end is not a strong type of nail by any means. If the nail is, conversely, very short and broad, broader than it is long in fact, you have the critic who will argue for the sake of arguing and who also has a quick temper. These people will give you a dog's life unless you are a really tough person who can find other uses for a frying pan. After all, it is the women who are supposed to have a monopoly on nagging.

If you find this sort of nail on a broad hand that is short in length, thick with nobbly joints on the fingers and thick thumbs, you are looking at a sadistic type of character who has served his apprenticeship as a nasty little boy, grew up to be a Billy Bloggs and went through a phase of quite enjoying nipping and pinching people. You won't see many of these hands about, but once you've seen them you won't forget what they look like, or feel like for that matter.

If you like conversation, try a man whose thumbs bend back at the tips; he'll talk about anything, and he's sociable and will probably spend his last penny on you. Of course if you want sensible conversation, try the one whose first finger is longer than his ring finger, but make sure the tip is nicely rounded or tapered.

This one can discuss for hours and is probably a schoolteacher anyway. Of course he can be on the dry side, so far as conversation is concerned, but really dry conversation comes from the chap with the very long middle finger, especially when it looks thin and knotty at the joints. This type makes a good analyst. The trouble is he's probably analysing you! As a career these types like the sciences, and analytical chemistry is the sort of thing that turns them on.

Now, take a nice long ring finger, a little longer than the first finger – this type has a slightly warmer, more personal conversation. If this finger is very long, almost as long as the middle finger, they may be a little scatterbrained, but they are warm, human, like to get along with people on the personal level, and they like nothing better than a garden fence to lean on – this is the ideal speaking platform for them. A little finger of course prefers the front parlour, but you'll know all about that.

If you like a man to do things around the home (and what woman doesn't?) there are two sorts to choose from. One is the spatulate type of hand. Perfect ones are rarely seen, where the wrist end of the hand is narrow

25

and seems to broaden out as it spreads out towards the fingers. The most common form is simply the spatulate tips to the fingers. Look at the first joint of the finger, and at the end of the nail it has the appearance of being very broad along the part you have to cut. The flesh at the nail tip is spatulate, the tips seem to fan out slightly.

On the ring finger, they'll favour a bit of cooking. On the middle finger decorating is their forte, but generally if all the tips have spatulate ends, they'll even have a bash at repairing the television. These types are curious and ingenious, like to find out how things work and even turn their hand to inventions. One thing is certain, this man has lots of energy; he is restless and always fishing around for something to do, so if you want to keep him out of his neighbour's house, garage, allotment, make sure there is plenty to fix around your own home, otherwise he may wander.

The other sort who likes pottering about the home is the owner of the more effeminate type of hand. Now this one you have to watch, he's inclined to set up in competition. It stands to reason that if his hands are more beautiful, i.e. effeminate, than yours, he is putting you out of a job. Don't under-rate this type; if the hand looks that effeminate they can be fantastic at flower arranging, planning, interior decorating, dressmaking, and will even do your hair. It doesn't necessarily follow he's less of a man because of this. Fundamentally, their sense of taste, evaluation and appreciation is high. They can usually spot originals from copies, play the piano beautifully and have expansive and cultured personalities.

The Venus mount tends to show the ambitious qualities in a man. For vitality it must be full as it protects the underlying artery. Without this vitality your ambitious man is a dreamer. The Life line encircling the mount of Venus must be well defined to show determination, and sweep well into the palm to show expansiveness and generosity. If it's straight with the top end rather high, going towards the first finger, he's a bit of an egotist, but he'll make his own way in the world. Sweeping out past the middle of the wrist indicates a strong constitution, good recovery from illness, an out-of-doors type who likes to travel and one likely to live a long time.

With a well-developed mount of Luna your man has good foresight and can plan ahead constructively. If the padding is thick near the wrist, fine, he'll plan ahead for you too, and will be more inclined to wine and dine you, take you dancing and whisper sweet romantic words in your ear. With a straight edge to that side of the hand under the little finger he can even anticipate your thoughts. If the edge of the hand curves out, this shows his originality. Not only will he be enthusiastic about your ideas, but he'll also add ideas of his own.

If the base of the hand is very broad and very narrow across the knuckles, you have a sweet-natured man who is fond of his own physique and may be a bit of a showman, which isn't so bad as they normally have the physique to go with it, where the base of the hand is also fleshy and firm.

If the middle of the palm is the broadest and well padded you have the good organiser, but one who can be stubborn and dig in his heels. Broad across the knuckles and heavy-boned from the back is a dynamic personality with too much uncontrollable energy. In a coarse hand this will indicate anything from a boxer to a psychopath. So be a little wary about choosing this type of character.

Finally, you will want to know who is going to wear the trousers – this one's easy; look at the palm of your hand, close your fingers together and your thumbs up to the side of the palm. How far up the third phalange of Jupiter, the first finger, does your thumb reach with the hand straight? Now compare it with your boyfriend – how far does his thumb reach? The winner wears the pants.

Don't worry about the length of the first finger – this is the one you wag at people when you are threatening them. Don't worry about the little or Mercury finger. This is the one you twist people around. Just consider the thumb because this is the one that decides the will power and who wins in the end.

So you can see much can be learnt by a simple examination of the hand shape, sometimes using your intuition and sometimes just ordinary common sense, which is not so ordinary as one might think and is sometimes sadly lacking in people's lives.

3 Basic Characteristics of the Hand

It is a leisure time for you, no one will disturb you, you are sitting comfortably with your partner. You are all set to find out some helpful things about yourselves. You are not trying to prove anything, you are going to enjoy a new interest. Probably if you get along well with the project, you'll get to know each other much better, there will be a new and interesting dialogue, which can be pursued over quite a long period of time, and a new line of enquiry into how each ticks; some interesting things can come to light and now you can set out into a more detailed way than we have pursued up to now, but hopefully quite as fascinating and enlightening.

GESTURE
Gesture is nearly always for starters; this is how you get to know each other by the handshake which accompanies the introduction at some social occasion. There is often the type of man who will grip your hand, drawing you perceptibly towards him while he gazes imploringly into your eyes, like a spaniel pleading for food and recognition. Few of you will fall for this blatant blandishment, unless the man himself particularly appeals to you – after all, you could never be sure after marriage he was not doing the same thing with an endless stream of ladies.

It is likely that the handshake that appeals to most people as an introductory gesture is normally warm, welcoming, but not a heavy grip. The owner of this handshake may appeal; you can go on further to see.

Sometimes you will meet the extra extrovert type, whether male or female, whose handshake will leave your hand utterly crushed and having to adjust slightly to get out the crushed feeling. These are people whose energy and drive would be better used on the sportsfield. If you fancy a breezy, extrovert and sporty type, pursue this further.

Occasionally, not too often luckily, one does have to accept a rather weak and flabby handshake, which leaves one feeling puzzled that the fact and the handshake do not match. The weak flabby handshake may be due to lack of energy, or to a psychological withdrawal from contact with others – 'it's really too much trouble' type of feeling. I feel that few people would be initially drawn to this type of person.

There is an even worse handshake, though, where only the fingers are offered, the palm remains uninvolved in the gesture. Not too wise to pursue this type further for the perpetrator of this handshake is an egotist, pure and simple, dislikes involvement, sharing or anything where there has to be a giving of self. Friendship or partnership? – the future looks bleak.

CONSISTENCY

When you shake or hold your friend's hand you will get the feel of it, its consistency; is it hard, flabby, firm, soft or elastic? It is of course easier to discover this by gentle pressure on the hand. Consistency generally answers the question – how energetic is this individual?

When the hand is flabby, the flesh crushes together easily and the energy level is rather low – doing is not this person's forte. There is a need for a stronger, more achievement-orientated partner. If the hands are also thick there is likely to be a lazy, self-indulgent aspect to the nature, which is fine if you're prepared to do all the planning, executing and general work around the place.

Where the hand is soft, there is of course a sensitive refined attitude to life, although there too the energy level may be slightly lacking.

Elastic hands are so called because they tend to spring back under pressure. Here, the energy level is excellent, these people are dynamic and seem to have a continual fund of energy.

Hard hands are usually found on men, rarely on women. The skin is also rather rough or coarse and people often have the character to suit the skin. These people have energy, but tend to inhibit it, not expressing it freely, which does little to help their health. They do not adapt easily to new ideas and so are very set in their ideas, attitudes and ways. Not too encouraging a picture for the would-be lover!

So, to sum up, the person who has rough, dry skin, skin diseases apart, is less sensitive and cultured than the person whose skin is smooth or elastic to the touch. It follows then that a more subtle, romantic wooing will be necessary in successfully making a friend or lover of the smooth fine-skinned type. The sensual, sexy side will not be so important as it will be to the coarser skin type, or to the type with thick hands. The coarser the skin the more inhibited the person in terms of giving of himself; he grows the skin to protect himself from any weaknesses such as a display of emotion. He is a prisoner of his own limitations, self-imposed generally, too.

TEMPERATURE

Another thing which is easy to ascertain on our road to understanding ourselves and our friends is the temperature of the hand which is offered to you to shake or hold. In practice, I have found that, if I remark to a client, 'My, your hands are cold', the return remark will be 'Cold hands, warm heart'. Do not be fooled by this old saying, as it is strictly not true. Naturally, if you've just come in out of the cold your hands will also be cold. But, after a short time in a normal room temperature, the hands will warm up, unless of course yours are always cold – some people tell me this and feel it is a praiseworthy factor, like having large and beautiful eyes. Not so, though; at best it shows a selfish disposition, at worst it can show a cold and uncaring nature as well.

FLEXIBILITY

An important factor to note as you give the hand a little more scrutiny is flexibility of fingers and thumb. Where the fingers bend backwards slightly when you grip the hand, your own or your friend's, and push the fingers back you can be sure there is a certain amount of mental flexibility. The mind is open to new ideas and will adjust and adapt normally to change.

Where the fingers when pushed back go right back, like someone bending over backwards, you will find that the person whose fingers do this is very impressionable, easily influenced, sensitive and changeable. A malleable nature which can be too easily led. The partner needs to be strong and yet flexible, knowing his own mind and so able to bring some stability and security into the life.

Where the fingers when pressed back do not respond, but remain obdurately in an upright position, you know this person dislikes deep-seated change of any kind and is also impervious to new ideas. His own, or even his father's, ideas are good enough for him. He is the traditionalist, he wishes to maintain things as they are, he dislikes compromise, seeing it as the wedge which might open the door to new ideas which could bring adverse changes. Unless you also have these attitudes, it seems many people would feel such a relationship would be too restrictive. Of course, he has the advantage of being steady, reliable and predictable . . . .

LENGTH OF FINGERS

We shall be going into the hand shapes later (these show the basic character as you will have seen in some measure in earlier chapters), but at the present time we'll just look at the meaning of long or short fingers (see Figure 3). Of course, if you were doing a professional hand analysis you would be measuring the length of the fingers and so determining with some exactitude the measurement of the middle finger which is generally taken as a gauge for length; the average length of the middle finger is about three-quarters the length of the palm, if the finger is longer than this it is considered long and if shorter than this it is of course considered short. However, you are using your eyes to assess this matter.

Figure 3

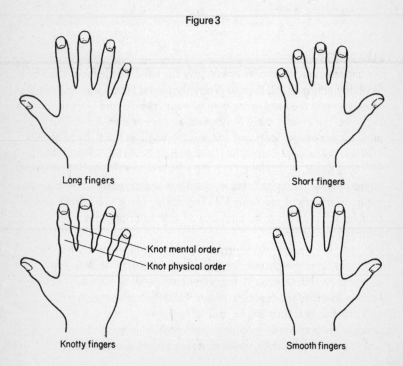

Long fingers

Short fingers

Knot mental order
Knot physical order

Knotty fingers

Smooth fingers

The longer the fingers the more meticulous and careful the person can be – they will not mind doing anything which has to do with detailed work. They are also thoughtful types and take their time considering any proposition. Their work would be marked by care and exactitude so they are not really the best mates for those impatient little quick-fingered types. Careerwise, they make fine mathematicians, physicists or statisticians, especially if the fingers are also knuckled.

Their opposite character is the short-fingered type. They are quick, impatient of delay and red tape. They work from intuition and instinct. Wonderful planners and organisers, they are doers rather than thinkers. If you want something done in a hurry, get together with a short-fingered type. They easily get bored with too much repetition and unless the palm is very square will swiftly move on to the next project leaving the detail to be worked out by the patient, long-fingered type, who incidentally may sometimes be unable to see the wood for the trees; that is, find it difficult to sort out what is really important and so pursue many blind alleys. The short-fingered type has faults also; they can be too impulsive, and get themselves into things which they really do not wish to pursue. They have such quick minds they expect everyone to be as quick; fortunately they generally get along well with others so any problems can be sorted out easily.

Long palms are, like long fingers, more thoughtful, often less materialistic than the short-palm type, who are very practical and able to organise their lives so that they receive a good reward for their work.

On the whole the study of Palmistry is for those long-fingered types who love detail, as every little thing is important. In a way the same type of person who would make a good researcher or detective Sherlock Holmes. It is being observant and noticing little things, particularly in the relationship of one finger, setting or pattern to another, which makes it such a fascinating study. It is the little things that matter.

FINGER SETTINGS

If you are still sitting comfortably then I suggest that if you have not already done so you have a table between you and that one of you shakes your hands from the wrists in order to relax them, then places them flat on the table. You will see from Figure 4 that the fingers form certain arches because of their different settings on the palm.

The most usual setting is one where the fingers form a gentle curve or arch (Figure 4a), the first and the little fingers being just that little bit lower than the middle and Apollo or ring fingers. These are well-balanced individuals, they rarely fly off the handle and are generally tolerant and easy-going. Remember, though, that you must never take an indication whether good or adverse by itself and without any corroboration from other factors in the hand.

Figure 4

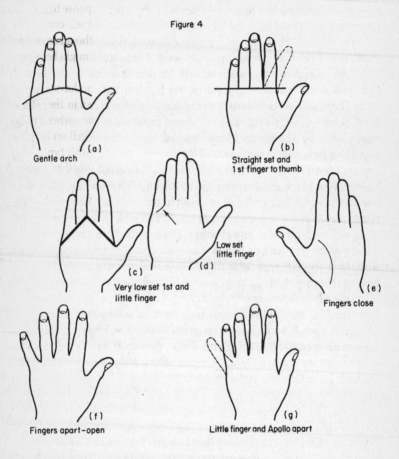

(a) Gentle arch

(b) Straight set and 1st finger to thumb

(c) Very low set 1st and little finger

(d) Low set little finger

(e) Fingers close

(f) Fingers apart—open

(g) Little finger and Apollo apart

Sometimes you will find that the fingers are all set on the one level, very straight across the hand, no arch this time (Figure 4b). These types are generally full of self-confidence and generally go ahead believing that everything they do is right and every idea or attitude they hold must be correct because they hold it. By being so cocky, they can court unpopularity, as they are so sure of themselves that they do not allow others to hold views which are contrary to their own without argument and maybe, given the right circumstances, even aggression.

There is another setting where the first and little fingers are both set much lower than the two more central fingers (Figure 4c). These people are often difficult to deal with as they have developed a 'poor me' response to life and so can be very defensive. Their belief in themselves and their self-confidence are low. These are things which it is difficult to put right without some form of therapy, so unless you wish to be defeated at every turn it might be a good thing to give this one a miss.

Finally, there is a very common setting with women who have after all been the underdogs for many generations and it still shows in the hands. Only the little finger is noticeably lowset (Figure 4d). The owner of this setting has a deep-seated lack of self-confidence, which is well set into the unconscious. The partner needs to build up and encourage this type.

Where these indications exist on the hands the person, whether male or female, needs a lot of understanding and support to make something of themselves. Their problem is that probably early on in life circumstances were not conducive to their optimum emotional and mental development; therefore later in life they lack that belief in themselves and in their ability to cope which is necessary to a happy, healthy and successful life.

If a couple who both suffer from this same syndrome of lack of confidence get together, and this is very likely, they can help each other to develop more confidence, but one or other may be too cautious so that neither develops their true potential. If one of the parties is flowing over with self-confidence, this may be too much for the shy, cautious and possibly rather fearful partner. If the confident one can carry the other for a while without overwhelming the more diffident partner, this could be a good and fruitful relationship. The giving would not all be on one side; the less confident one also has something to give and to teach the other to their mutual benefit.

While finger setting is an important indicator of basic attitudes, so also is finger spacing; but here we have to remember that the latter are for the 'now', their placing represents the present situation, i.e. how the person feels today, whereas the other, the finger setting, is generally for keeps, comes from the past and extends into the future.

FINGER SPACING

In order to view the finger spacing our relaxation exercise is once again needed. Once again one of you shake your hands so that they hang quite limply from the wrist once you have shaken them for a second or two. As in the previous exercise, one of you will view the finger spacing while the other is of course the guinea pig, then you will change over. If possible remembering to mark the results of your exercise in your little notebook.

The idea of shaking the hands from the wrist to relax them is quite important as it means that, when you hold your hands up for inspection, the backs facing your friend please, the fingers will fall naturally into their proper places giving you the correct psychological interpretations for the present time.

When all the fingers are spaced well apart when your friend holds up both hands for study (Figure 4f), you'll know here is a lover of independence, someone who is open, generally extrovert, outgoing and vital. There will be a certain childish quality, for children when asked to hold up their hands to be viewed will, if they are happy and developing normally, hold them up all spaced out. Of course this type can make a few enemies as being of an independent turn of mind they speak their minds without fear or favour, and not everyone likes this way of approach, certainly not if they are the recipient of criticism.

The first finger being apart and held towards the thumb (Figure 4b), we know this is a person who likes to lead, to travel, to make up their own minds on things. If the ring finger is apart from the middle finger there is no great dependence on the partner if this indication is on the left hand, or on working with others and having their support if it's on the right hand. The little finger's stance away from the ring finger (Figure 4g) shows a fair dislike of too much responsibility, a need to put some distance between the self and the family at times. Freedom of action is craved. Above all this person has confidence in self, in life and in the future, but they do not want to be tied down, their keywords are freedom and independence. A man must not expect her to be solely the little woman in the home. She could not fill this bill; she needs also a wider field and one where she'd not only enjoy a career, but also make some money for herself, to support her desire for independence in the financial field as well.

The opposite stance to this, in terms of spacing, is the person whose fingers are all held tightly together (Figure 4e). Immediately you will get the feeling of restriction and inhibition as you look intuitively at the proffered hands; you are absolutely right, too. There is a strong reserve, and an introverted outlook on life is probable. The person needs support both in emotional and financial terms, and may still be dependent on the parents or if married on the partner. This person values security above all. It may be that you are looking at the hands at a time when the person has suffered some crisis or loss, and is not normally so fearful, insecure and worried. Remember the finger spacings are temporary and generally represent a present picture. So it's necessary to take in present circumstances and events when trying to assess personality and its ramifications.

The person whose middle and ring fingers are closely linked together has one deep inner need and that is for domestic peace and happiness, the security of a happy home life with an understanding and co-operative partner. The home must have good furnishings and things of beauty and value. If you can supply these things and also need them yourself, it seems this could be the right partner for you.

FINGER JOINTS

There is another factor which is of interest to you both in your assessment and this is the smooth or knotty finger joints. This can be assessed as before by shaking the hands and lifting them up for friend to see, the backs outward.

A swift glance will satisfy you whether the fingers are smooth or knotty (Figure 3). With the smooth-fingered folk, ideas flow easily; there are no blocks as are represented by the knots. These cause the flow to stop awhile and consider the situation before flowing onwards again. The very first knots between the fingernail and the first joint are said to be knots of mental order, so the ideas will be very well arranged and presented. The second knot is called the knot of physical order and refers to neatness and tidiness in a physical sense as applied to the concerns of the finger on which it is found.

If both these joints are protuberant then you have a thoughtful philosophical type of person who likes to analyse every important situation carefully. Their conclusions will be given after due thought. The finger type can also belong to the precise technician, and these people are much in demand in today's complex industrial world of technology.

If only the second knot is protuberant these people must have a pleasant and ordered environment, disorder can make them very unhappy and ill at ease. Where they find it in other people's places they are not affected, but if the place is their own home or workplace this is different, they need a tidy and ordered environment.

THE THUMB

We can really say that the success of man in manipulating the world to his advantage comes solely from his being endowed with a viable and working thumb; something which no other animal possesses. Because it opposes the fingers, man has been able to use tools and subdue the world, making some of it worse and some of it better, but mainly working solely for his own benefit without due regard for the earth itself, or the other inhabitants. Hopefully as people become more conscious in a realistic way this will change for the better and greater consideration will be given to all the world's inhabitants.

In a personal sense the *thumb* is the most important member of the hand. Indian palmistry considers that the thumb alone can give a pretty good character reading. Look carefully at the thumbs to see whether they are in proportion to the rest of the hand. They can be too heavy or too small and so either put too much pressure on the personality or too little. In fact too much accelerator or too heavy braking can be going on, conducive to neither happiness nor success.

Broadly speaking, *thumbs* may be divided into those which are *firm and long* (Figure 5a), and which when pushed down resist pressure, and those which are soft, pliable and back-bending (Figure 5b). The owners of the first thumb shape have firm, realistic, rather unbending characters. They do not adapt themselves to you, you adapt yourself to them or you make off fast to the woods to recover from the encounter. They make good friends, though, and bad enemies. If either type of thumb is held close to the hand (Figure 5c) they tend to be uncommunicative as well. This is because they trust few people, none until they know them, so they don't tell you very much at all. It is rare for the pliable back-bending type to have thumbs which cling close to the hand, and the attitude is then usually a temporary one.

If the thumb is long, that is comes up to or nearly up to the first joint of the forefinger when you align it there, then you have quite a tough character. If the two joints or phalanges are equal (Figure 5d) then you have a perfected strength of will, excellent reasoning power and great capacity. They can achieve what they set out to do. The top phalange symbolises will power; the second phalange reasoning and logic; and the third phalange at the base of the thumb is the mount of Venus and reveals the individual energy and warmth of feeling, including of course sexual energy.

If the top phalange is short and bulbous (Figure 5e), beware – this person has a temper and blows his/her top at times. Generally, this is inherited from one of the parents or imbibed in childhood from the offending parent.

If the *second phalange is longer* than the first, you'll have endless discussions re any proposed change; this person finds it hard to come to a decision, especially if the phalange has a nice smart little waist too. Endless pros and cons crop up and are pursued in depth, so that eventually the whole project may die of inanimation.

If the *top phalange is longer* than the second then expect to be eternally picking up the pieces from decisions taken on impulse by your friend.

The *backward-bending* thumb is really nice (Figure 5b), it shows a generous and flexible nature, someone who'll be cooperative and easy-

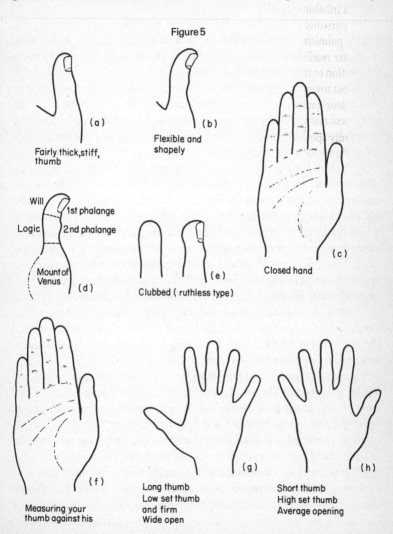

Figure 5

(a)

Fairly thick, stiff, thumb

(b)

Flexible and shapely

(c)

Closed hand

Will — 1st phalange

Logic — 2nd phalange

Mount of Venus

(d)

(e)

Clubbed (ruthless type)

(f)

Measuring your thumb against his

(g)

Long thumb
Low set thumb
and firm
Wide open

(h)

Short thumb
High set thumb
Average opening

going. Problems of adjustment will be easily met. Remember, though, that the backward-bending thumb, especially if it really looks like being double-jointed and a whizz at aerobics or yoga, is not nearly such a strong thumb; it lacks the persistence of our earlier example, but it is easier to live with generally. The backward-bending thumb bestows one disadvantage, in that its owner loves to spend money, and so if you haven't any or your money is hard won you may dislike this scene a great deal.

The wider the thumb opens (Figure 5g) the more extroverted and way out the person. Someone who likes to be the boss and for the world to know it; so, if you don't like to play second fiddle, choose someone whose thumb opens to an average 45° angle (Figure 5h).

Reserve and a more introverted attitude is revealed by the closer angle to the hand (Figure 5c). Sometimes fear, insecurity and inhibition cause the person to keep such a tight rein on themselves, or some trauma or crisis has caused a temporary feeling of insecurity. Once this is past the thumb may well return to a more relaxed angle.

In practice, I notice that if the person is unhappy then the top phalange turns inward. If it's on the passive or left hand then you know the unhappiness relates to personal life; if on the active or right hand then the problem is related to the career.

The ideal thumb seems to be: a) one which complements the hand on which it resides; b) one which is long, i.e. when measured comes up to the first joint of the forefinger; c) one which is not heavy or too bulbous at the tip; d) one with a fair balance between the two top phalanges, so that action is neither inhibited nor too impulsive. The owner of this thumb, other things being equal, should be a great success and also find personal happiness. The owner of the shortish thumb is likely to have difficulty in making decisions. These people often find that life is carrying them along willy nilly without their having much say in the matter.

We mentioned earlier that the longer the thumb is the stronger the will; so, if when you measure (Figure 5f), your friend's thumb is longer than yours, testing both against their appropriate first or Jupiter fingers, then you've found the one who'll have the deciding vote in your relationship when anything important is at stake. If the thumb has a shapely look and the tip is nicely rounded then the will power will be persuasively used, and if of course the little finger is also long and shapely, you'll never understand how it is that you so seldom seem to win, but of course the charm level is so high that you probably won't really mind all that much anyway.

4 Hand Functions, Types and Traits

Once again you and your friend are sitting quietly and peacefully opposite one another with a small table in between. The first thing we are going to appraise is harmony or disharmony as shown by the relationship of the various parts of the hand to one another. Ask your partner to hold up their hands first of all with their backs facing you, then reverse the process and ask for the fronts to be presented. What is the first thing which catches your eye? Maybe a large thumb on one hand and not on the other, or again you may notice that one hand is larger or in some way different from the other. However, your main observation should tell you whether indeed the hands are good to look at, present a harmonious face to your questing gaze, so that no part of the hand is over or under developed, and above all the fingers should be straight. As a student of hands I will always remember our very famous tutor, Miss Beryl Hutchinson, telling us 'Hands are best worn straight'. I've forgotten many things since, but this will always stick in my memory. Remember, crooked hands have crooked owners. It is that simple; in this case your hands are a dead giveaway.

Pleasant-looking hands, with good proportions, will minimise their owner's negative traits and so of course make for pleasant companionship.

RIGHT HAND/LEFT HAND

Before we go on to any other hand divisions or descriptions, we have to note that in right-handed people the right hand is the objective conscious self, the one we present to the world as ourselves; it could be said to represent the Ego in a very general sense. It corresponds with the left side of the brain, the logical, practical, mathematical side which would generally appear to be more masculine-orientated. It is said that extroverted types are objective in their appraisal of life, so we can call the right hand the objective hand. The left hand reveals our imaginative, intuitive, emotional side, the more passive, subjective, feminine side. It corresponds with the right hemisphere of the brain. This is because the messages which we receive from the brain are crossed over as shown in Figure 6a.

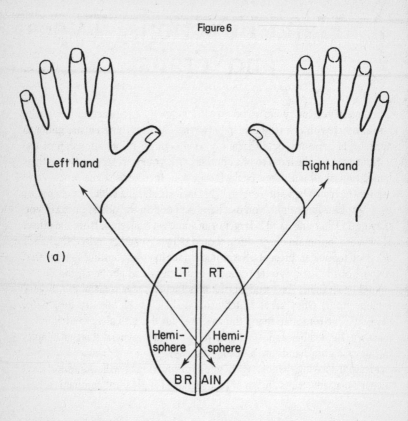

Figure 6

(a)

Of course this layout has to be reversed for those who are left-handed. In their case the left hand will be the positive, objective Ego self and influenced from messages coming from the right side of the brain. The right hand will be influenced from the left hemisphere of the brain and will represent the more intuitive, passive, artistic and feminine or subjective side of the person.

We can now divide the hand itself first of all vertically. Hopefully, your friend the victim is still around and you are willing to enjoy a little drawing; unfortunately this can leave your friend's hands in rather less than a pristine condition, for, as many of you will have guessed, the writing or drawing is

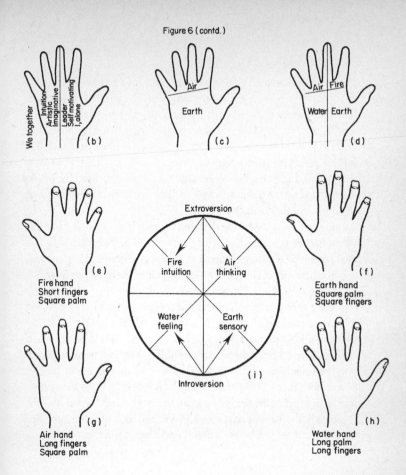

Figure 6 (contd.)

(b) We together — Intuition — Artistic — Imaginative — Leader — Self motivating — I, alone

(c) Air — Earth

(d) Air Fire — Water Earth

(e) Fire hand
Short fingers
Square palm

(f) Earth hand
Square palm
Square fingers

(g) Air hand
Long fingers
Square palm

(h) Water hand
Long palm
Long fingers

(i) Extroversion
Fire intuition — Air thinking
Water feeling — Earth sensory
Introversion

not to be on the wall but on your friend's hands. So, with the hands before you, draw a vertical line from the middle of the Saturn finger to the middle of the wrist, just as shown in Figure 6b. Look at the two sides; are they equal or unequal? If the thumb side of the hand is the bigger, then this person has a positive, objective, logical, rational attitude towards life. Here you have the leader type, one who gets things done, sees things through, is self-motivating, and makes his own decisions. We might call this side I ALONE.

If the ulna or percussion edge of the hand side is the more developed then you have someone who is more intuitive, sensitive, imaginative, artistic and subjective. We might call this the YOU TOGETHER side. This operation should be done on both hands in spite of the moans of the victim, your friend.

There is more to come, and having assessed the above and noted it in your little notebook or on your notepad, you now draw a horizontal line under your friend's fingers and assess whether the fingers or the palm are most developed (Figure 6c). If it is the fingers, marked Air, then the intellectual forces are strong; if the palm is the longer, the person is more practical. The reason for this is that the palm brings us down to earth; the fingers can jump about as they will, but in the end to get anything done they need the power potential provided by the palm, so as you will see we have marked Earth on our second horizontal division of the hand.

We can now put together in one drawing the two diagrams we have just done on your patient partner's hands (of course it will be your turn soon). In Figure 6d we combine the four elements as they are symbolised in the hand, so to the right of the vertical line, on the thumb side of the hand, we have Fire and Earth, and on the other Air and Water.

Just before we give you the characteristics of the four elements give one overall look at your friend's hands and mark down whether you consider the feel of the hand and its proportions to be harmonious. At this point in time you are being asked to be perhaps more intuitive than you usually are, or maybe you are usually gifted in this way, in which case you are fortunate.

There have been many ways of dividing the hands into types in order to help classify and so order the study of human nature through the study of the hands. Classically there are seven types and we shall look at those later, but using the four elements can be both useful and illuminating.

TEMPERAMENTS
These are grouped according to a fourfold classification.

The Fire hand
The Fire hand (Figure 6e) is warm, strong muscles are present and the lines are sharply outlined. Fire is the power of life, makes possible energy and activity. Fire people are enthusiastic, inspired by interests and ideals, active and aggressive; they push forward into life.

Of course fire needs control, as out of control it can cause destruction not only to itself but also to others and to the environment. Discipline and control are necessary in order to use the Fire power effectively. You can

44

understand that the Fire type needs space, and plenty of challenges in order to live, grow and make progress. If it grows over-cautious, its wings are clipped and the impulse and initiative which represent its way of operating remove its power and free-flowing life. Lived negatively it can be insensitive and finally the destroyer, but its real role is to be the leader and the winner in life.

Compatibilities
Other Fire types. Air attracts too.

The Earth hand

The Earth hand (Figure 6f) has one main characteristic – its inflexibility. It has to be inflexible as it is the element which guarantees stability and continuity in a changeful world. The Earth hand is usually strong, broad, firm and bony. The skin is rough and dry with very few lines. There is no leaping striving as in the Fire hand, but a calm, solid, progress which moves slowly and gradually onwards and upwards. Chances are not taken; this is the hand of tradition and respect for the past and the future. Like the earth itself it provides home and sustenance, is reliable, conscientious hardworking, disliking change and sceptical of anything considered to be new-fangled or gimmicky. Things and people need to prove themselves to the Earthy type who values experience, tradition and the past.

On the negative side this type can get too stuck in a rut, can refuse innovation, which improves life, such as electricity on a farm, for instance. They can be prejudiced without reason about things they do not understand.

Compatibilities
Other Earth types. Also Water people.

The Air hand

The most notable thing about the Air hand (Figure 6g) is its flexibility. It is nearly always on the move with nervous gestures signifying restlessness and the desire to be where the action is. Its keenest desire is to be free, hence the Airy types are hard to catch and perhaps even harder to hold. There is sweetness to be found in life and the Air type wishes to find it all and to enjoy particularly the delights of the mind. The stirring bit of news or information . . . .

Air folk do not wish to be deeply involved in life as this would mean both responsibility and commitment and the Air hand wishes to be free and untrammelled to go here there and everywhere there is interest or innovation. Air fears to be tied as it is like being imprisoned. If it's emotion you're after, don't look here. The Air type, as you'll have gathered, finds emotions difficult to manage, so often they prefer not to try, but everyone has their Achilles' heel and this is theirs. Air can unite, the soft word that turneth away wrath, it can also stir up trouble and strife. Those whose work lies in communication have a big responsibility in reporting the news.

Air hands can be recognised by their fine fingers, the many fine lines on the hand which do have some direction and the dry skin.

Compatibilities
Other Air types. Fire people and even Earthy types.

The Water hand
Water is Being, yet it has no power of itself, it reflects and mirrors. It is a large part of our own biological being and so very much part of ourselves, our instincts, our early years, our dependence on our parents for life and sustenance. Water has its magical, mystical side, we gaze into water as we sit by the waterside, we see the landscape mirrored there, sometimes the reflection is true, sometimes distorted. Water washes away our physical dirt, it cleanses us, but it also washes away our sins as in baptism, where new Christians are welcomed into the Church.

Water has many different faces, we can meet it as snow, ice, water or steam. Water extinguishes Fire, it is equally hard on Earth, eroding it quickly or slowly according to time and pressure. The predominantly Water type (Figure 6h) needs protection and organisation, some sort of structure to contain it and make it feel safe and secure. In love it can be sacrificial and look after the invalid and the small child, devote itself to the family needs above its own. Negatively it can be weak and lean on others, living life at second hand.

The distinguishing features of the Water hand are that it has no structure, it is damp, often a trifle plump with 'little holes' instead of knots, there are many lines and they appear to have no direction. The skin is fine and often shiny.

Compatibilities
The Earth type is best as it gives structure, organisation and so containment to the Water person who will then feel much less insecure and 'drifty'.

Now, you will really be saying to yourselves first of all 'Which type am I?' Remember that pure types are rare, so judge predominance of a certain element. Then of course you'll be considering the predominating type of your partner.

The Fire type in love

The Fire type in love is fiery, positive, enthusiastic and impulsive. They like to make progress, otherwise can lose interest fairly quickly. Life with the Fire type is rarely dull, but there is an objection to routine so don't expect too much of the same in the home. Exciting new ideas and places to go come before the cleaning. Life must be challenging and work should give scope for initiative and invention. These types sometimes lack sensitivity and consideration. There is little you can do about this, it is often part of their nature, like blue eyes and red hair are physical characteristics. It may be that there is a little bit of insensitivity or selfishness in your own make-up in which case you can get your own back in your own time and at your own pace . . .

Compatibilities

The Fire type gets along well with other Fire types for they understand one another well, they can attempt the impossible together. Their endurance level will be doubled and indeed they may make the headlines for some wonderful deed of valour and 'derring do' which just catches the roving camera eye. Just as the Fire type does not like to be tied down into too structured a relationship, so such a fate would also lack appeal for the Air type; so Fire and Air could well go along nicely together in understanding one another's need for freedom.

The Earth type in love

Earth types never do anything without due consideration and would rarely do anything so important as getting married without giving the whole matter careful consideration. Security is always important though, and if getting married or having a permanent relationship would bring more stability and security, then the Earth type will look around for a suitable partner. Some Earth types will choose purely for a comfortable, well-run home with children. Others will marry for status, money or ambition.

Never the most demonstrative of people, the Earthy types have deep feelings and need understanding from their friends and partners. They understand that love is not mere saying 'I love you', but proving it by effort to make life better for the beloved. In most cases the wife and children of the Earthy type know he works to achieve satisfactory status, security and stability. This type is conventional and if reasonably happy in the marriage or relationship will not wish to make changes and will settle easily into the domestic routine. They will accept restrictions, embrace responsibilities and show no special sorrow for loss of freedoms. The marriage or long standing relationship has to be very unsuitable before any consideration would be given to divorce. Children and their responsibility would weigh heavily in favour of continuing the status quo. You will have gathered that speed of thought, innovation and demonstrative romantic actions or ideas are not really part of the Earthy type's repertoire.

Compatibilities
In view of the above, the other Earthy types would seem to be a good thing, as ambitions would be shared and attitudes to life and love would be similar. Also excellent would be the Water types, as they would contribute softness and sympathy and, especially where the family and love are concerned would help to bring out the protective side of the nature.

The Air type in love
As mentioned earlier, emotion is not the easiest of feelings for the Airy people to express, or to hold onto once they have found it. The reason for this is that on the whole they tire easily of people and interests and need a continuous supply of novelty and mental stimulation. If you want to hold your Airy partner or friend, do not get too demonstrative, demanding or restrictive. They'll simply walk away from any situation which might prove too emotional, or where a tantrum or quarrel is blowing up.

As these are light, intellectual people, they can be held by sharing interests and mental stimulation. They do not appreciate the need for security as the predominant thing in life, they prefer to take a chance.

Compatibilities
Other Airy types would make for the happy sociable scene so beloved of these people. Adaptability and originality are also plusses and available with Air types. The Fire types will also attract and make good friends and partners, supplying the enthusiasm for a project and warmth of feeling often rather lacking in the Air type.

The Water type in love

Make no mistake, these people are sensitive, timid and love to protect or be protected. They are not independent because of their fear that they will be left unprotected and alone in a hostile world. They like to link themselves with stronger types and be supported by them. In fact they are often rather passive. They love their homes and families, are rather suspicious of outside influences until they know and trust them. They like to choose their own friends and to have a lovely secure, warm family circle. As these are not independent people many hang onto marriages or relationships far too long when nothing really holds them together, except perhaps that the finances do not stretch far enough to allow for separation or divorce. Children and home as providing shelter for the Water type's need to feel protected and to protect are the two important things in life.

The Water type is particularly good at sensing other people's feelings, and this intuition may be so strong as to amount to psychic ability. So kindness, understanding and sympathy are Water type virtues, their vice is that they can be too possessive, dominant and demanding emotionally.

Compatibilities

Other Water types who easily understand the sensitivity, fears and timidities as well as the anxieties over family and loved ones. Otherwise, the Earthy type gives a more practical look at life and provides structure and protection for the rather timid Water people. The latter can often be better than two Water types who might get bogged down in their own fears and so become too cautious for their own good.

This division of the hand which I have given you is based upon the new typology which the great Swiss psychologist, C.G. Jung, devised. The four types were Air (the intellectual, thinking type), Fire (the intuitive type), Earth (the sensation type), Water (the emotional type). I have found this works very well in explaining people to themselves or to their partners through Palmistry. Jung stated that most people have a dominant attitude in their approach to life, which is one of the above mentioned types, but if your friend will once again oblige for you to check and if you will look at Figure 6i you will see that the thinking type is opposite the feeling type and the sensory opposite the intuitive type.

Jung's theory states that if one state is dominant then the opposite one is always less developed. He also said that the thinking and feeling functions are selective. The thinking function is rational, so also is the feeling function, so we make judgements and shape our values from what our feelings tell us.

The two non-rational functions according to Jung are sensation and intuition. He mentions that, when we think, it is in order to reach some conclusion; when we feel, it is in order to attach a proper value to something. Whereas with sensation and intuition we perceive something. In terms of sensation we perceive, say, the smoothness of the table or perhaps some other more pleasant sensation. Where intuition is operating then we perceive through the unconscious. Most people have one dominant attitude, with the function which is opposite to the dominant function repressed, that is, not easily expressed. For example, the *thinking type dominant* will have feeling repressed. However, all is not lost, for while it is difficult to be perfect, that is with all four functions operating equally effectively, we do have compensations. There is a compensatory or secondary function, which will not be in conflict with the dominant function. In this case it would be either intuition or sensation and either of these will complement the main life attitude.

From this short exposition of Jung's typology, you can see for yourself what is likely to be your friend's main attitude to life from finding the type and also the least developed of the four functions in your friend's life. When it comes to your friend's turn to do this for you the same will apply.

Over and above these, Jung stated that people's attitudes were either extroverted, and so linked to objects outside of the self, which might be called an objective attitude; or else introverted and therefore subjective; or an attitude which is related to the self; i.e. the world exists basically as it appears to me as well as in itself, or how it appears to others. We all know the extrovert; pleasant, optimistic, easy to get along with, sociable and cheerful. We also know the introverted type, quiet, reserved, often silent and withdrawn. So finally we might say 'so-and-so is a thinking, intuitive, introverted type'. We shall look at introversion and extroversion later on, as there are many ways in which they can be seen in the hand.

I recommend that you and your friend have a nice relaxing break now, after all the concentrated application you have had to put in on this chapter.

5 Traditional Hand Shapes

Hello, nice to know you are still with us, welcome. In this chapter we are going to refine down a bit the four basic dispositions given in Chapter 4. The reason for doing this is because it makes it easier for us to understand ourselves, our friends and lovers, which on the whole is the main object of this book. Probably, most of you will agree that very little progress in life can be made without relationships, which fulfil a deep need in everyone's heart for understanding and sharing, both the good and the bad in life.

HAND SHAPES
There are three hand shapes which form a sort of upward progression.

The Elementary
The palm is square, the fingers short and the skin rough and leathery (Figure 7a). You will gather that this is an unevolved type who can be very good in a situation requiring physical skills such as boxing, wrestling, driving machinery, farm working. He is good with animals, but is not as you will have gathered a great communicator, or the world's greatest lover. In fact as he lacks imagination and his scope in life is limited, the bad type of Elementary turns to crime, so watch it if you find one of these on a 'blind' date.

Frustration is their bugbear so a friend or mate would need to try and understand and reassure the many insecurities, which can make this a dangerous and violent person.

The Square hand
This much resembles the Earth type which we discussed previously. It is given the name 'Square' because the palm is literally square, that is the width is the same as the breadth (Figure 7b). This type like the last and the next is

Figure 7

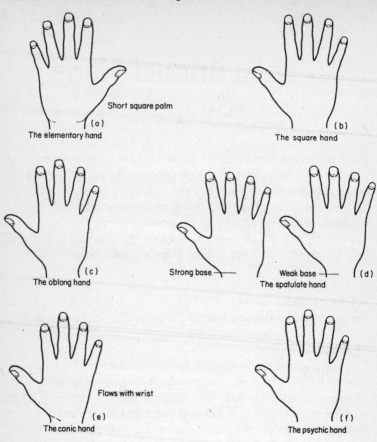

Short square palm

(a)
The elementary hand

(b)
The square hand

(c)
The oblong hand

Strong base — Weak base — (d)
The spatulate hand

Flows with wrist

(e)
The conic hand

(f)
The psychic hand

more often seen on male than female hands and is very down to earth, practical and hardworking. Steady, solid, reliable types, they like their lives to be well structured by routine.

Within this structure the Square feels secure. He likes to know where he is, where he stands and tradition is the name of the game. Innovations or innovators are not to be trusted, they could bring chaos into his carefully ordered and constructed life. The Square is for you if you value someone who is utterly to be trusted, completely reliable, and responsible. Someone who will not leave you alone to cope with two tiny children to bring up, but who dislikes change, who will be possibly maddeningly regular in his habits – the 8.45 am and all that, returning at 6.30 pm exactly each weekday. Someone not very demonstrative or given to romance or drama. However, you will find Mr Square is correct and diffident when courting. He's unlikely to look for sex outside marriage and, even when married, he would dislike any variations on a theme. In fact, he is inhibited both emotionally and sexually. If you are Miss Conic, then you'll have your own way once you are Mrs Conic, and not before, of changing his sexual habits slightly, but not very much, not very drastically. Do not expect a Don Juan to spring from out your Square husband's breast. It just won't happen, but if you accept him as he is and remember he'll never be sparkling, you could make a happy little family.

If of course you are a Square lady then you are made for each other having the same fundamental disposition.

The Oblong hand

Earlier on, I mentioned that the first three hand shapes I would discuss would go in a sort of upward progression, so this one marks the top of our progression. The Oblong palm (Figure 7c) gives the character more scope, and routine with good time schedules and excellent structure is not so necessary for security as with the Square type. Therefore, as a lover or husband, he'll be less inhibited emotionally and sexually, more flexible and willing to try innovations. His job can also be more interesting, demand more of him and so widen his ideas and general life attitude. Another Oblong or Square would suit; a solid relationship would be the outcome, both partners practical and realistic.

Although I have suggested that the possessor of the Elementary, Square, or Oblong hands is very often male, this is not of course inevitably, or always the case. There are females who possess Elementary, Square and Oblong hands. In general the skin texture is rather dry and rough, there are not many lines on the hand, the flexibility of the hands is not great, which would suggest that there is less sensitivity than some other types; the lack of flexibility points to a dislike of change and innovation, and also of new ideas so that the female of the species, in this case the Elementary, Square and Oblong types, can have a certain tendency towards masculinity, which with other indications which we shall discuss later can lead on to lesbianism.

The Spatulate hand

The Spatulate is restless energy incorporated (Figure 7d). If the spatulacy comes from the distal or finger end of the palm then it is the ideas type you have on your hands. Often the follower of causes, the guru hunter; everything is mental and stimulating, the more way out the ideas the more attractive. However, remember with this type the base is weak and so the hand (the person) is not very well grounded in reality in the practical affairs of the here and now. If the spatulacy comes from the wrist end of the palm, then the person may well be an inventor of useful gadgets, or with a liking for going off on projects which take him/her away for months at a time. This person has loads of physical energy, while the other has loads of mental energy. Neither type are very impressed with the ideas or ideals of the last few types we have been examining. Security is not their priority. It is an interesting changeful life and a partner or friend to share things. The Spatulate likes to be free to do interesting things with their lives and grudges too much drudgery.

Spatulate with Spatulate would go well, or else Square with Spatulate. Both are energetic people, like to get things done, the Spatulate more creative, innovative and original, the Square more practical. The good things attached to this combination would be that the Square would help to ground the Spatulate's ideas. However, there may be some difficulty here in that Spatulate may find Square a bit of a ball and chain, a hold back. Probably, the greater flexibility and broader ideas of the Oblong would suit the Spatulate type better, and vice versa too.

While one can say that up to date we have discussed psychological types which seem to suit the male best, it is obvious that if these are found in a female it would suggest a more masculine approach which has implications in career, outdoor or masculine careers being preferred and now more often chosen by women. It also has implications in terms of love life and choice, which will be gone into later in more detail. While I hope that my two friends are still with me, I wish I could have the use of a telescreen in order to flash on it at once these various hand types with a short description of their meaning. However, this is a dream and cannot now be a reality, so we must content ourselves with what we have and accept our limitations, but I hope to make the hand types as simple and easy to pin down as possible.

The Conic hand

We come now to those hand types which might be termed more feminine in shape, the first of which is the Conic (Figure 7e). There is a rounded, pleasant shape to the hand, no hard lines or sharp edges as with the hand shapes we have already discussed. Adaptable, intuitive and loving change and variety, the Conic hand does best working with people, in some job where charm, diplomacy and organisational skills are needed. For instance a PR job would be excellent. Often she'll have linguistic or artistic skills which can bring interesting career opportunities. Similar opportunities often crop up in the Conic's love life; she can turn on the charm whenever she fancies anyone or anything – so if you are male and have a new Conic girlfriend, beware . . ..

Loyalty is not Ms Conic's first or even second name, the desire is to live and enjoy life to the full, and this includes sensual pleasures and indulging sexual desires. Boredom is something to be shunned at all costs, so you need to keep on your toes if you wish to keep in with this glamour puss. In marriage, Mrs Conic likes to think her man is desirable and is not beyond discussing his various sexual prowesses with her girlfriends, the aim being the enhancement of her own personality. Of course this also applies with a boyfriend or boyfriends.

The male Conic, like the female, sets quite a store on charm and glamour, many go into the entertainment world, into art, design or hairdressing. Both male and female like money and what it can buy and so set out to have a high standard of living. Both tend to require some boost to their self-esteem which they seek from the opposite sex, but if the home is satisfactory then the straying will simply be casual and both will return to the fold.

The Square in love and marriage is loyal, predictable and hardworking, one might say a jewel of a man or woman, but as change or a disturbance of the routine rather frightens the Square type so it's hard for him to succeed independently in business. If married to a Conic, this problem disappears, for the Conic will encourage her husband to go ahead and build his own business, will have lots of ideas and will give support. Together they can go places and succeed.

The Spatulate, like the Conic, hates to be bored, and if the extra width is at the base of the hand a lot of energy is channelled into sport or adventure of a physical kind like leading a group to Kashmir or climbing mountains. Most male Spatulates are like that, restless, energetic innovators, independent and original. The Conic and the Spatulate can get along quite well, but the Conic has to accept that she is not likely to be the centre of her husband's life, and he may often be off on wonderful, engrossing projects.

Like the Square, the Oblong would find a good mate in the Conic, both giving each other something the other lacks. The Oblong being less routinely inclined than the Square, can prove less frustrating to the impatient Conic.

The Oblong would also be able to tone down the impulsiveness of the Conic type, which so often lands it in trouble.

The Psychic hand

This is a pretty recognisable hand for our two friends, whom we will hope and assume are still with us. It is a longer and thinner edition of the Conic (Figure 7f). It has a slender fragility. There are two types: one has a soft crushable hand, the other is slim, hard with twisted claw-like fingers. The first is a walkover for the unscrupulous lover. Romantic, idealistic and totally out of this world, this type of Psychic needs protection and a kind, honest lover or husband. The second type is the opposite, the hard-handed claw-like Psychic takes other people for a ride, takes everything she can get and is cold and calculating at all times. She plots and plans to get her own way and generally does.

The soft-handed type is very insecure, but still would not consider marrying for money or status alone. For her, love and warmth are important. For the hard-headed, claw-like type of Psychic the opposite is true, she is out-and-out for herself, and she chooses the husband who will give her the mostest in terms of this world's goodies. In return she gives as little as possible. We have to remember the Psychic hand is so named because those who own it are psychically gifted and very intuitive, so that even the hard-handed type knows how to get her own way and how to protect herself. One thing is certain – Psychic should not marry Psychic, this would be disastrous as neither would be practical enough to make a go of married life. If there are children, they'll generally be spoilt or smothered by the soft-handed Psychic; the hard-handed is generally far too selfish to have children, but if they do they generally palm them off onto someone else to look after. The husband of the hard-handed Psychic is really the one who suffers, having chosen such a vampire for a wife; and if he's a loyal Square or Oblong then its hard for him to extricate himself easily from his mistake.

Probably the best mate for a Psychic is the Conic who will match the Psychic in sensitivity, be creative and adaptable and provide something practical and realistic for the Psychic, so that ordinary everyday life could go on without the general chaos which the Psychic left on their own can produce. Either the Spatulate or the Square would be asking too much in the way of adaptability which neither really have.

My dear friends who have been following these work-outs can probably now do with a rest after examining their hands in the light of the different hand types shown earlier.

FINGER TYPES

We now have to go onto looking at the different digit types. Splitting up the palm and finger types makes it easier to compare these and so to decide on compatibility on a wider base. As you will see later we shall be 'peeling the onion' more and more, and so getting a really good view through seeking answers at different levels. I hope this will be interesting to my patient readers; at least relatively painless and informative.

We discussed the various finger lengths and types in Chapter 4, but now if our two friends will once again seat themselves either side of their table so as to be able to examine their partners' fingers, and in making these exciting comparisons glean more information about each other.

Compatibility of Finger Types

1) *Short fingers with short fingers.* Here speed and impatience will mark the attitude to life of both parties. These are intuitive types who love everything to happen the day before yesterday. It's likely that some mistakes will be made because of the speed at which things will be done. In particular, decisions may be made on impulse and so without due thought. Life will be interesting and enjoyable, never dull.

2) *Long fingers with long fingers.* The opposite to the above types. Here, care and attention to detail would mark the attitude of both parties. Decisions would be made slower and after due thought. The parties would understand one another well, but life could be a little dull and drag a bit.

3) *Long fingers with short fingers.* A fairly difficult proposition, but if other facets of the character concur the two natures could well be complementary, each partner producing what the other needs. The short-fingered person would be quick, impulsive, intuitive, able to set things up and get them organised, but needing the attention to detail to keep everyday matters going along satisfactorily. It would help if hand shape was the same; if not, the partnership could well be short-lived.

4) *Knuckled fingers with smooth fingers.* You will remember that smooth-fingered folk tend to be spontaneous and speak their mind without too much deliberation, whilst the knuckled folk are analytical and thoughtful. These two types have, therefore, two different attitudes to life, so may well get on each other's nerves, probably much criticism coming from the knuckled partner whose mind is geared in that direction anyway.

5) *Thin fingers with thick fingers.* Thin-fingered folk are in general more able to eschew the delights of the flesh than are thick-fingered types who are generally more materialistic, sensual and lovers of life's 'goodies'. The thinner finger types may have more self-control, be less attracted to material things, or have a spiritual or ascetic attitude; whatever the reason the difference exists, but is not an insuperable obstacle to joint happiness. If some sort of compromise can be reached where hobbies and interests are concerned there are possibilities in this link-up.

6) *Weak thumbs with strong thumbs.* You will remember we discussed thumbs weak and strong in Chapter 3; the thumb represents the Ego and the willpower. The stronger the thumb, the stronger the character; the weak thumb gives away a weak character. These are often people who feel that they are just borne along on the tide of life without being able to influence their own lives very much. It is true that sometimes the less strong type is drawn to the strength of the other more dominant character. This is particularly so where men are concerned as generally their life role asks them to be more positive and dominant. In the past this allowed for much dominance on the part of the male and a weakness verging on masochism in the female. If we keep going too far and too fast we may now reverse the roles to everyone's detriment. These two might get along well if they complement one another, the one partner being the leader, the other the led.

7) *Open fingers with closed fingers.* If you remember earlier we suggested that you ask your friend to shake their hands from the wrists and to raise them up with their backs to you, the fingers straight up. If the fingers once raised are separated then you have a free spirit, one open and friendly, extroverted and sociable. If all the fingers cling together you have an introverted personality, closed, cautious, withdrawn and reserved. These two types do not get on over a period of time, unless there is a sort of fading in and out of the type, i.e. there are times when your friend or partner is introverted and times when he/she is extroverted. Few people are completely definite types, there are more usually shadings to be considered.

6   The Mounts

The mounts are little raised hummocks on the hand. There are nine of them and they are named after the planets. Each planet represents a facet of character and so its representation in the hand depends upon its size and location. See Figure 8a for the names and location of the mounts. The centre of the palm is known as the *Plain of Mars*, and above this, starting under the forefinger, is the *mount of Jupiter*; then under the middle or Saturn finger, coming from right to left, is the *Saturn mount*; the *Apollo or Sun mount* is under the third or Sun finger; lastly, the *Mercury mount* lies under the little or Mercury finger. Beneath the mount of Mercury lies the *mount of Mars Negative*, and continuing on down the side of the hand lies the *mount of Luna*.

Figure 8

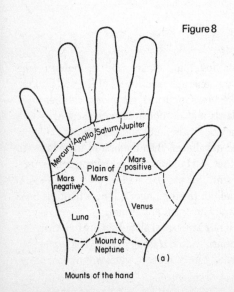

Mounts of the hand

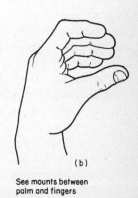

(b)

See mounts between
palm and fingers

The *mount of Venus* is really the third phalange of the thumb and takes up quite an area of the palm, with the upper part under the *Jupiter mount* being the *mount of Mars Positive*. Between the *Venus* and *Luna* mounts at the base of the palm lies the *mount of Neptune*.

We have to understand that these mounts represent energy stored nice and neatly to be used by the owner when required. The higher and firmer the mount, the more of that particular type of energy exists for use, and the more dominant the mount the more the person will show of the particular characteristic attributed to the mount.

It is easier for you and your friend to examine the mounts if the hand is bent a little as shown in Figure 8b; this particularly applies to those mounts under the fingers. Incidentally, many palmistry books will tell you that the mounts should be directly under the fingers, for example, the Jupiter mount should be directly under the Jupiter finger; not so, the correct position for them to protect the nerves underneath the skin is for them to lie between the fingers, so that talk of 'displaced' mounts as being in some way a minus factor is incorrect. Mounts have to be displaced in order to perform their physiological functions.

A mount can be well-developed, over-developed or deficient, so, my friends, begin to get your eye in to judge the mounts of the hand. This is not difficult and can tell you quite a lot about your friends and acquaintances.

THE MOUNT OF JUPITER

Jupiter was another name for Jove, a Roman God of bounty and beneficence. Jupiter's children are generous, and lovers of life and giving. They are also leaders and achievers. Good to their wives, children and families, they have high standards and do not hold with those who fall below certain standards of achievement, honesty and nobility.

If the *mount of Jupiter* is *well-developed*, then the best of these honest, just, optimistic and sociable virtues will be shown by the person concerned. Leadership qualities will be present.

If *over-developed*, and especially if the forefinger is longer than the Sun finger, then the attitude is probably arrogant and proud.

If *deficient*, that is the mount is not a mount at all but simply flat, then the person lacks confidence and enthusiasm, no staying power. The Jupiterian with a well-developed mount makes a good partner, gives without counting the cost, has a sunny disposition and can be depended upon to see a project through having much faith and confidence in providence and in himself.

The over-developed type needs to give more consideration to others. The deficient mount needs a partner who can encourage and give support, otherwise little will be achieved owing to lack of enthusiasm.

THE MOUNT OF SATURN

Another name for Saturn is Chronos, or Old Father Time. Saturn is the teacher and often teaches us many hard lessons; therefore, it is always said to give seriousness to the nature. It is also situated at a point where the meeting of the conscious and unconscious lies in the hand. It is therefore concerned with balance and adjustment. On the whole it refers to our attitude to our responsibilities, to occult studies and on a lower level to the material factors in our world. The Saturnian often has musical ability or keenly appreciates good music. They can also be seekers after wisdom.

If the *mount of Saturn* is *well-developed*, you have a serious personality who is concerned with seeking wisdom. If not a 'loner', he has some need for seclusion from time to time. He also possesses a well-developed sense of responsibility.

If *over-developed*, with a long Saturn finger as well, you may have someone who is introverted, too much into themselves, cold and rather distant.

If *deficient*, then you have the happy-go-lucky type who does not take anything too seriously and is not afflicted by worry.

There is one sure thing you can say about a Saturn type, even well-developed: he's got lots of common sense. He will always put duty and responsibility first, so remember he can be a bit cheerless and stolid with a well-hidden sense of humour. He does not improve with age.

While the Jupiterian is the marrying kind, many Saturnians do not marry, preferring a solitary life, and really they are not very attractive with their rather mean habits, their duty-first stuff and their wet blanket attitude. I suppose one can say that they have their good side, which is that they are usually responsible, reliable and save money – however, they may have to be dead before you get your hands on it.

So, if this is the dominant mount in your friend's hand, you'd better think seriously about getting involved further; if you do you can expect to continue to do so for the rest of your married life.

61

THE MOUNT OF APOLLO OR THE SUN

Apollo was the Greek God of the Sun and so radiates joy from the person who has a good well-developed mount of the Sun. Here we have a sociable nature, creativity and the ability to give joy, to write and speak well and to be a positive presence on the social scene.

Well-developed, the Sun type has warmth, optimism and radiates a presence which encourages others and gives to them in a positive way. Any 'blues' are quickly chased away.

People rejoice to have this type around and the Sun-type household is a busy active one with people involved in community work, in the entertainment field, in government office, and perhaps in sport with its various activities and interests. Sun-type children like to hold the centre of the stage, and the adults need a partner they can trust and respect. When respect flies out of the window so does love. As a lover this type is versatile, intuitive, and appreciative of beauty at all times. Often a dress sense is inborn, knowing what will look right and suit you as well as himself.

If *over-developed*, there is a brashness and an insensitivity, with big talk,but little to back it up. He sees himself as brilliant and successful, particularly in love, boasting of his conquests. This is more often found in the male than in the female. Let's hope you are not taken in by this type and find yourself repenting at leisure.

Just as the well-developed mount gives warmth, a loving nature, and an ability to make a happy relationship or marriage, the *deficient* mount is said to denote a cold and cynical nature and a lack of appreciation of the finer things of life. However, remember not to judge character on one quality or the lack of it. It is possible that a great love can awaken the nature to life's possibilities and its creative side.

THE MOUNT OF MERCURY

Mercury, whose other name is Hermes, has always been considered to be the winged Messenger of the Gods, and so rules communications of all kinds from business matters to books, papers, neighbours, short journeys, and information of all kinds. In fact, the mount and finger of Mercury, although the smallest finger, is a sort of compendium in the number of matters it rules. Basically, though it has to do with the owner's intelligence and method of expression, whether through speaking, writing, singing or creating beautiful poems.

When you're dealing with a Mercurian you're dealing with just about the fastest thing on two legs with a brain of quicksilver to match. Lovely at parties, the *well-developed* Mercury mount type really adds zip to your party; people love to have them around, as they provide such good company and entertainment for everyone – nothing serious, though, you understand. They love to travel, to be on the move, to have a life of excitement and change. Probably the best bet where marriage is concerned is another Mercury type, whose work and hobbies are similar, so that there is plenty to talk about. Where both have the same type of life the general fear of the strongly Mercurian type that they'll be caught like a butterfly in a net is assuaged.

Generally, the Mercury type gets on well with young people and likes children, but the children must be mobile and able to travel wherever the Mercury type happens to be working. A word of warning; don't try to imprison this one into a dull routine, it just won't work and you'll be the loser.

If *over-developed*, i.e. where the Mercury mount is over-large and the Mercury finger is also either twisted or bends inwards, you can have the consummate liar who is not even honest to himself. He has rationalised to himself that everything he does is quite right and proper because he could not do otherwise, or some other type of mental 'let-out' enables him to live with himself. The words charming, glib and cunning come to mind in considering this type. Fraud in business and cheating in love are quite common. It's not unusual for the person to be running two love affairs at once or more often one wife and one mistress. Because the Mercurian has such a convincing line in chat, he manages to get away with it, often for a considerable time.

Where the mount is *deficient*, it is likely the person is either shy and diffident or just plain dull, although it is possible that the latter effect is the result of the former inhibition.

I am hoping that our two friends are still with us and are finding the mount comparisons easy to follow and informative. The mounts we have been studying because they are situated in the upper and more active part of the hand are easier to define in terms of expression than are the mounts which are situated in the more passive and instinctive part of the hand. These are the mounts which we shall look at now.

THE MOUNT OF VENUS

As mentioned earlier, this is really the third phalange of the thumb and its area is encircled by the Life line, which tells you that this is the indicator of power and vitality. What type of energy? Perhaps a better question would be: how does this person use his energy?

Well-developed
As this mount is called after Venus, the Goddess of Love, we can tell that this mount has to do with our appreciation of art and music as well as our capacity to give and receive love. Here we have warmth, vitality and lots of energy. So this person is fun-loving, has physical charm and grace and may love dance or athletics. The energy present makes it possible to resist disease, or to recover quickly from any affliction.

In love the Venus-type is warm and giving, especially if the mount is nice and springy. A firm, full, well-developed mount is tremendously important in love, for here is someone who has much to offer both sexually and in terms of companionship and social life. There will also be enough energy to make a good life for the family, to actually earn the necessary money to run the home with a good standard of living. Time and energy to play with the kids and to enjoy their company too for the Venus-type loves life and living and makes a good husband or wife.

In terms of compatibility the full-developed mount type and the flat or deficient mount type will be totally incompatible – just miles apart, for the developed type has of course a nice wide life which flows richly out into the hand and gives the broad giving Venus mount so essential to a loving and giving relationship, satisfactory on an emotional and physical level.

Deficient
Here you will find the Life line as (see Figure 8a) closing in the mount by huddling in close to the thumb; there is a lack of vitality and so inability to be passionate or sincerely warm and giving. The person is liable to be cold and rather selfish or self-concerned. Unless you are of this type yourself and who would own to it, stay away, for this person will use you to their own advantage and you'll end up disillusioned.

Over-developed
The keyword here is *too much*, for the over-large Venus mount type is too greedy, too intense, too ambitious. The good qualities of the Venusian are exaggerated, overdone, all too much. However, as he is never satisfied his ambitious desires are likely to carry him to the top of his profession and you with him, should you marry or have a permanent relationship.

If the mount is also soft then you have the sensualist who loves all the good things of the flesh, including the sex pots; so if you are not an extremist where sex, drink and food are concerned leave this one alone, for you never know where this search for sexual and sensual thrills is going to lead in the long run.

In general one can say that if the mount is *ordinarily developed* we have the expression of *physical energy*; if the mount is *deficient* then we have the expression of *mental energy*; and if the mount is *over-developed* then we have the expression of *emotional energy*, mainly desire on the various levels it operates.

Another thing I'd like to mention is that the Venusian knows what he/she wants and goes after it with some success.

THE MOUNT OF LUNA

This is situated opposite the mount of Venus above the wrist (see Figure 8a). As you will note its home is the unconscious, passive part of the hand. It is above all the storehouse of memory. Childhood, ancestral, racial, all sorts of memories are stored here. Here we find the source of all our unconscious drives, our imagination, our fears and our repressions. As it is a storehouse, it is the reservoir of all creativity, the strength of the writer, his storehouse of goodies upon which he can draw. It is possible that here we have the memories which go back to the womb of this life and, for those of you who believe in reincarnation, beyond this into the mists of our own earlier times on earth.

Well-developed

If this mount is full and firm this person will know what he needs to survive and achieve. He can plan for the future, being able to envisage the end result of his visions. The future of the world has been dreamt up in someone's unconscious and put into action by someone's energy and persistence. Writing and creative ability are present, especially with a sloping Head line which ideally would be divided under the Apollo mount. We can also say that a strong Luna mount gives a compassionate, caring, nature and so the desire to look after and care for others, as in nursing or any social or community work, even work with animals. This latter is particularly emphasised if the hand sports 'samaritan' lines under the Mercury finger as this gives healing ability.

Deficient

The person lacks imagination and understanding of others, is rather dull company and lacks a sense of romance, so is not for all those girls with lovely Conic or Psychic hands. If it's also higher up the palm than the Venus mount, then it gives a venturesome nature, racing drivers, rock climbers and those who take insane (to ordinary folk) risks; they don't worry, so enjoy fast cars and other risk-taking of all kinds.

THE MOUNT OF NEPTUNE

The Neptune mount lies at the base of the hand between the Venus and Luna mounts (see Figure 8a). An interesting mount, for it encloses both the conscious and unconscious areas of the hand, marking as it does the dividing line between the two; an added factor is that it is situated in the passive or instinctive side of the hand. Neptune is a nebulous planet, it is mysterious and enchanting, and lends charm and a hypnotic allure to the person who has it well-developed.

Well-developed

You cannot mistake this mount as it links Venus and Luna and presents quite a high ridge at the bottom of the palm. It is excellent for actors, who need to captivate an audience and move them to tears or laughter at will. Speakers or lecturers with a well-developed Neptune hold their audience and get a good name for being most interesting, no matter what the subject.

Deficient

Although possessing a well-developed Neptune gives that extra cachet to speech and character, its absence or deficiency does not imply that the person will never make a speaker or actor, since there are other factors which give a helping hand to these professions, such as a good Mercury mount and finger giving the gift of the gab. A good Jupiter mount enables a person to project themselves confidently and successfully so without this, there may be difficulty in putting over a message or some very good ideas.

I hope that my two friends have found the examination of each other's hands where the mounts are concerned of interest, and now have a greater understanding of the many factors which go to make up the complex character of the modern human being. In the next chapter we shall examine the various Mars mounts and their meanings in terms of love and relationships.

7 The Mars Mounts, Love and Sexuality

In the last chapter we looked at all the mounts except the Mars mounts and the Plain of Mars. Having had so much to consider, my two friends may now need a 'second wind' to understand the mounts and to look at those which we have not already considered, but I think that you will both find it worthwhile and gain much fun and enjoyment from it too.

In life we seek balance and this can only come if energy is used constructively; the amount of energy at our disposal is shown by the various mounts of the hand. The names of the mounts are of very ancient tradition, as helping man from earliest times to understand himself by categorising and naming the gifts of the Gods and representing them symbolically in the palm of the hand and fingers. Even more convenient than relying, as does Astrology, on having to make up a birthchart from the time, date and place where a person was born, as here the chart of the psyche was present for all to see and for the interested parties to learn to decipher the meanings set not in the stars but in the hands.

Traditionally, the idea was that the life force or energy entered through the fingertips and from there infiltrated the various mounts, so the higher the mount the more the energy gathered there. As we have seen, each mount represents a specific force at the disposal of the person, and therefore endows us with talents and abilities which are ours. There are certain mounts which refer more directly to love and sexual life than others and we shall look at these from this point of view.

MARS NEGATIVE OR UPPER MARS
This mount lies under the Heart line at the point where it is under the Mercury mount (Figure 8a). Its lower boundary is a line drawn from the thumb to the percussion. To view this mount you'll need to look at the side of the hand (the percussion). It may be thick or thin or taper off into the

hand. The well-developed Upper Mars mount endows the person with courage, persistence and determination, an ability to quietly keep on keeping on. We may often be presented with situations which require this much courage and persistence. Conditions of hardship, crisis, long illness of one of the parties! The person who has this mount well-developed can face grave and sometimes lengthy situations and come through in one piece.

If this person gives love it will be enduring; there is loyalty and the loved one will be defended and protected at all times and in all situations. Could be jealous as there is a wellspring of feeling.

If this Upper Mars is *deficient or missing*, where the same area as above is flat, then there is something missing in a moral sense. The character is sometimes weak, the thumb short and thin, the hand narrow and the Heart line short, stopping under Saturn, some factors we shall look at later, then we have someone lacking in loyalty, in a feeling of respect for themselves. From the marriage point of view they are not a good bet. They would be likely to be easily influenced by whoever made out they were interested. They'd cheat in the marriage or relationship because their sense of self respect is missing and often they are selfish as well. Stay away unless you relish being let down and worse.

MARS POSITIVE OR LOWER MARS

This mount is situated, as you will see from Figure 8a, in the upper part of the area surrounded by the Life line which encircles both the Lower Mars mount and the Venus mount. Being situated in the conscious part of the hand it is energy which is used in an open, aggressive or martial way, often impulsively.

A *well-developed* Lower Mars mount suggests this person has courage, self confidence and is well able to stand up for himself or herself. He's nobody's pushover. It is naturally something sports types need to compete and win.

Obviously, courage and energy are necessary for us to make a success of life and love. The person with a well-developed Positive Mars mount will have the necessary drive to take you out, ask you to meet him more often and eventually propose. The type is more a masculine one than feminine, but it is one which is open and clear cut, no messing about; you'll know what is wanted and he'll put his cards on the table honestly. You'll know exactly where you stand. Being in love may well tone down some of the male aggression and temper it with sweet Venus, but you'll have to remember that this one is naturally, in some things at least, a 'loner', and can be selfish or self-centred.

The *deficient or weak* Positive Mars mount is not a leader, not self-confident, not able to stand up for self so obviously not to be counted on to stand up for you, or for any family you might have. You'd have to supply the courage and self confidence and might well hate your partner's approach to others, which can basically be summed up as 'peace at any price'.

If this mount is *over-developed*, i.e. very full and the first finger is shorter than the third, this person resembles my dog who always goes for anyone on principle, and I must stress when I say anyone in this case I mean any male of the canine variety. The short first finger shows the lack of self-confidence, the caution and the mistrust which often leads to aggressive acts. We have so many examples of this nowadays it is a waste of time to labour the point. So unless you wish to be continually listening to tales of how others got at him and caused him to act in such and such a way, which landed him in an argument or a fight, you'd best give this one a wide berth and concentrate on more pleasant company, which I am sure is offering to you right now.

In assessing the Mars mounts from the point of view of love and marriage, remember never to come to a conclusion on one factor only. Look at the other factors which may well influence your judgement. As you will recollect, the shape of the hands gives the basic characteristics of the person, the rest adds more information and so enables you to give a sharper, more correct interpretation.

THE PLAIN OF MARS

This is like a huge reservoir of energy right in the centre of the hand (Figure 8a) and like all reservoirs it has to have width and depth in order to provide the necessary when it is required. So, deep and firm, its owner is energetic, enthusiastic and healthy. He likes to be secure in the material sense and so sees that he and those close to him are well supplied with the good things of this world. In short one could call him a materialist, but healthily and happily so.

The traditional reading of a *thin firm* Plain of Mars is that this is a very unlucky symbol, and perhaps the old palmists were not far wrong; but they did not say who was unlucky, whether it was the owner of the thin Plain, or those who were manipulated by him. Very often in practice, the thin Mars Plain type is shrewd and manipulative as an expression of an inner insecurity. When my friends are looking at this situation they should bear in mind that this shows a basic weakness in the character, but judgement should be withheld until other things have been considered; if you still have your notebook, just make a note of the situation so far as your friend is concerned.

Now, the Plain can sometimes be *flabby* and *soft*, which suggests someone who is soft and self-indulgent, is not keen on too much hard work and so is to be avoided, as the partner will surely end up as the breadwinner and the general dogsbody.

If the Plain is *thin* and *soft*, in contrast to where it is thin and firm as mentioned above, then you have someone who is always doing things for others, the taker-in of stray dogs and cats; people with little discrimination who really should not be using their slender energy fund in such an extravagant way.

SEXUALITY
In our search for meaning in the analysis of hands we have looked at many possibilities in terms of affinity or incompatibility. Some of these we will go over now and we will examine new and interesting factors in assessment. The first of these is often sex. How sexy is my partner likely to be?

Sexual energy
As we have mentioned earlier, the thick powerful, firmly elastic hand is potentially sexy. If it is too hard, and especially if the fingers are also inflexible, then you have a cold and rather difficult type. Self comes first and others a long way after. This of course applies to sexual habits as well. We saw that the thin Plain of Mars showed a low energy potential and so there is also a low sex drive.

The thin, soft, narrow hand is also lacking in energy and so in sex drive too. The main indicator, though, of love, warmth and the ability to give and take in a relationship is the mount of Venus; if this is firm and sweeps out well into the hand you have plenty of energy and so potentially a good achiever sexually. The opposite is true too – if the mount is narrow with the Life line pulled in towards the thumb then you have someone who is not really interested in sex or passion, may in fact be rather cold and prudish.

Skin
By now you will know quite a lot about hands and so of course their owners. For instance, you will know, without being told, that it would be totally

incompatible for a lady with a fine skin and delicate hands to get married to a chap with a coarse skin. Skin, like hair, has its own texture, and the finer the skin or hair the more sensitive and impressionable the owner. This person has an appreciation of the finer things in life, is interested in art, music and culture. The ideas on what is acceptable sexually will not be purely on a physical sensual level, as it would tend to be with the coarser-skinned type.

The skin really represents the clothes of the body and might be conceived as being used for contact, yet it can also be used for protection, in which case a sensitive person might well develop extremely hard skin symbolic of the need felt for protection. In interpreting the hand the reader might assess the person as coarse from a genetic point of view, while the real reason would be an emotional/psychological one. The difference could only be assessed by talking with and understanding the person, for this defensive attitude would show itself fairly quickly in conversation.

Fingers and thumbs

We spoke earlier about the angle at which the *fingers and thumbs* in both hands are held, and these too will tell a tale about sexual attitudes. You will remember that, if the fingers are held together when the hand is raised for inspection by one of our interested parties, the person concerned tends towards an attitude of shyness, introversion, and insecurity. Remember that this attitude may be temporary; you may be seeing the fingers at a time when their owner is going through a difficult period in their lives. The same conclusions can be drawn with the thumbs; where these are held close to the hand there exists an attitude of fear and inhibition where sex is concerned. At best their owners like to have sex as a sort of ritual habit within the marriage bed of course – probably on Saturday nights with the lights off only.

The roots of this attitude will go back to childhood, to ideas and attitudes imbibed from the parents. Probably sex was never mentioned in the parental home, and therefore the child learnt by implication that it could be wicked, dangerous and must be carefully controlled. Of course they threw out the baby with the bathwater. Sex *can* be dangerous; we live in an age where this is made obvious to us nearly every day by the media, but this is because its link with love has been forgotten and that where two people come together in love the sex act is the final and complete fulfilment of their love.

Where the fingers are open you have a more extroverted, sociable, friendly type; with the thumb at a wider angle the person will not have crippling inhibitions because their view of sex will be different. Sex will be seen as part of love and marriage and the partners will seek to find fulfilment together.

Where the Jupiter or forefinger is longer than the Apollo or third finger, you'll have the forceful type, and with a woman this may mean she finds it difficult to play the feminine role; she may be the one who calls the tune, unless of course her partner also has a long forefinger, in which case there might be a tussle.

The opposite problem might afflict the male with both forefingers, and especially the passive forefinger, shorter than the third or Apollo finger (see Figure 1). He may well need a little encouragement from his partner as his idea of self is not as positive as it might be. It is generally the encouragement to get started which is needed in this instance . . . .

Where the Saturn or middle finger is very long you have a serious person, maybe someone who even takes sex seriously; if you both feel that way, things might take a very long time to get to a head, going through long years of courtship and engagement while the money is piled up slowly and laboriously. Unusual for this day and age, but quite common earlier in this century with less secure and affluent times. More common now apparently are the short Saturnian fingers, where very little including sex, marriage and children are taken seriously. One might comment here that these people are great at parties and at spending your money, or other people's.

Where the Apollo finger leans towards the Saturn finger as if it is embracing it, you have a clinging vine, so, if you're prepared to be the support, this can be a happy relationship or marriage where the one who wishes to be supported meets the one who wishes to support.

If you are out at a party and meet a girl with a ring on her right Apollo finger, she's definitely looking for a partner; the ring is her signalling this to those who know. This is even so if she also has a wedding ring on her left Apollo finger – message, she's thinking of changing him.

The little or Mercury finger is, as mentioned earlier, a compendium finger whose meaning embraces so many things, but one of those things is the sex drive. Is your partner sexy? This can be answered by the appearance of this finger. If your friend has a little finger which is long with a fine tip, a knotty second joint and a nice plump third joint next to the palm, your friend is definitely sexy and will respond well to your advances, provided they are in line with his/her wishes.

Another little item of interest for you, my friends, while we are on the subject of Mercury or the little finger, is to try to avoid someone whose *Mercury finger curls in towards the Apollo finger*; they tend to be puritanical. A *ring on the right-hand Mercury* tells a tale, that the pursuit of money has taken over from the pursuit of love. A *ring on the left little finger* shows either an over-concern for sex and sexual problems, inhibitions, if the finger lies close and curls in, or a dislike of closeness, a sturdy independence and often detachment, which veers on coolness, when the finger juts out. These attitudes do present obstacles to love and harmony in a relationship, but of course most things can be overcome if there is a desire to do so.

Figure 9

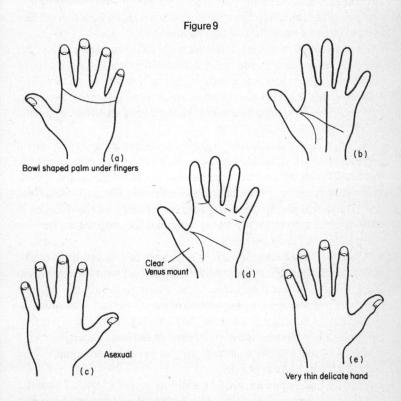

(a)
Bowl shaped palm under fingers

(b)

Clear
Venus mount   (d)

Asexual
(c)

(e)
Very thin delicate hand

OTHER SEXUAL PREFERENCES

There is no traditional way in which *homosexuality* or *lesbianism* can be found in the hand, but a certain amount of modern research suggests that there are two types:

1) the conditioned homosexual or lesbian influenced by feminism and political pressures (see Figure 9a);

2) the genetic type, one might say those who are 'born that way'. This type always has a very strong Saturn or Fate line cutting the hand like a knife in the left hand. Generally, the upper part of the palm is broader and there are knots on the second joints of the fingers (see Figure 9b).

In the first type, the conditioned homosexual or lesbian engendered by political influences, there is besides the factors present for the genetic type a much wider top to the palm where it joins the finger bases. These people are interested in a Saviour figure, such as the Ayatollah or any other ideological figure you like to mention. The top of the palm (see Figure 9a) is shaped like a bowl to receive these influences and blessings.

Very rarely you may meet those you might call *asexual types* where the interest in sex is minimal. You can recognise these by the bulge at the top of the palm on the percussion side under the Mercury or little finger, and there will be another bulge below on the Luna mount (see Figure 9c); also those with long thin hands and those with minimal lines on Venus (Figure 9d and e).

Although some palmists have suggested that the possession of a certain pattern (the whorl) on the Mercury finger is an indication of homosexuality, this is really just a sympton of the person concerned having no stable sex life. In a woman knots on the second joints of the fingers (Figure 3) would lead you to think that perhaps there was a lesbian tendency, or else of course in older women it may simply be an indication of incipient arthritis or rheumatism thickening the joints.

Where there are problems such as impotence or frigidity these can be medical or emotional; very frequently the latter. They stem from the way in which the person sees themselves. Often a change of attitude, the right therapist or healer, and the co-operation of the partner can work miracles, although if the condition has been of long standing one would expect it to take quite a few treatments before it began to respond. Generally, too, a change of mental attitude from negativity or pessimism to optimism and expecting the best works wonders.

Although this chapter has veered slightly off the beaten track, I hope our two friends or partners are still on their journey of exploration and finding new insights as they progress.

8 The Heart, Head and Life Lines

Dr Charlotte Woolff, who studied the hands of mentally-retarded children in her care, said that the lines showed the working of the brain, since there are more nerve endings in the hand than in any other part of the body. They were, so to speak, the outward signs of inward grace or the inner workings of the psyche (see Figure 2).

I realise, at this point where we are going on to examine the lines on the hands, it is going to be more difficult for our 'friends' and others who are following this exciting trip of exploration into ourselves. However, sit as you were, keep your little notebook by you; just have a new heading now, which should be LINES. If you have any difficulty in seeing or locating the lines mentioned just look carefully at Figure 10 and open the hands up gently to see the lines and their course.

You will see at a glance something important; the hand in Figure 10a just has the three basic lines – this is known as the *Empty hand*. The one in Figure 10b is covered with a mass of lines and is known as the *Full hand*.

Here we have two very different types; the Full hand's owner is nervous, worrying, impressionable, insecure, sensitive. We noted earlier that both the Air and Water hands were generally *Full*, while the Fire and Earth hands appeared to be more controlled and single-minded.

We have to remember that those people with Earth-type hands generally approximate to the Empty hands. They are people who have good nerves, do not worry too much and generally are possessed of a good sound constitution. They are of the Earth and at home here; they know how to cope with day-to-day problems.

The Full hand people, by definition either Air or Water types, do not find themselves in their own element here on earth. Their natural element is either the wonderful expanse of space, where their ideas can take wing without being impeded by the need to be practical and *down-to-earth*; or the Water type who have as their element the great rolling depths of limitless

75

seas, where they are as much at home as they are at ease in little shadowy pools of still water, where they can rest awhile. When we look at these two different types we have to remember their elemental background and then it is easy to understand.

Figure 10

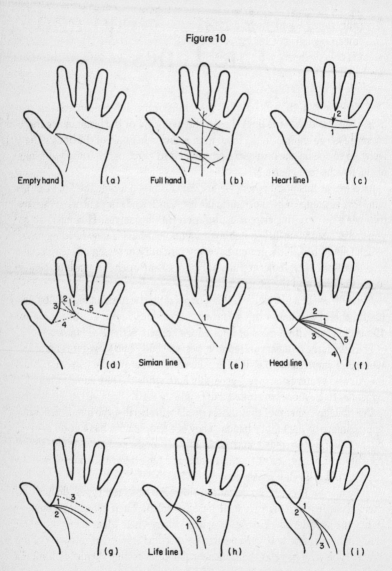

76

THE HEART LINE

Since you may well be thinking that the Heart line is the only one that really influences relationships, we will deal with this line first (Figure 10c). It is not true of course that the Heart line is the only one that matters when we are dealing with romantic matters. The hand as a whole matters, the shape, flexibility, skin texture and mounts; and now we are examining the lines and their meanings. Practically everyone has a Heart line, except those who have what is called a Simian line (Figure 10e), where the Head and the Heart line are fused into one line, running across the palm. The Heart line indicates our attitude to emotional matters, how we deal with our love life, our lovers, our husbands or wives and everyone we love and cherish, so of course all the most important emotional facets of our lives.

First of all it is necessary to say that the *ideal line*, no matter where it is located on the hand, is one which is visible and clear. Too fine or too broad and fuzzy are not good conveyors of the energy current. Like rivers the lines can be so fine they are incapable of coping with heavy stuff, or so broad and shallow they cannot take the tonnage which needs depth.

The Heart line is generally considered to start at the edge of the percussion under the Mercury, or little finger, and to proceed along its way towards the Jupiter mount or finger.

The reason for writing this book has been to help you to look before you leap (or wed). One of the most important indicators of compatibility is the Heart line, or rather the Heart lines of the proposed partners; probably it's easier if they match, but where there is goodwill and an understanding approach to the other's emotional needs, there need not be disappointment, even if there are areas in the hand which show dissimilar approaches to life.

Position

There needs to be a nice depth between the Heart line and the finger bases (Figure 10c1) giving warmth and feeling to the character; with this person the *heart rules the head*. If the line lies closer to the finger bases (Figure 10c2) then you have the *intellectual type* – the one who rationalises his feelings and ends up not knowing if or what he feels. If the line is also straight this approach to love can become calculative, i.e. what shall I get out of it; the gold digger can be of either sex. Not easy for these two types to get along together . . . .

Just as there are almost as many attitudes to love as there are people, so when you come to look at the Heart line you will see that its thickness, its

77

length, its position, its direction and endings can all vary enormously from person to person.

Length and direction

One can say that most Heart lines run from the percussion under the Mercury mount over to the mount of Jupiter (Figure 10d1), and the line rises up between the *Jupiter and Saturn fingers*. With these people peace and harmony in the home are what is desired. If this is not forthcoming, in spite of efforts made to achieve it, the person will withdraw into themselves and gradually the relationship will wither and die.

Where the Heart line *runs up high onto the Jupiter mount* (Figure 10d2), you have someone with great expectations, not only in terms of emotional satisfaction but also in terms of status, intelligence and integrity. If they are let down, they really suffer, for their need was great and their expectations high, perhaps too high.

Where the line goes right across the hand onto the *Lower Jupiter mount* (Figure 10d3) you'll be fine if you remember that your mate needs to work, and gains more satisfaction and fulfilment from this; and, let's face it, you take second place. Of course, *you* might also be wedded to your work, like two designers, two film stars or producers, or perhaps a couple of photographers whose work was absolutely fascinating. Things could work quite well, especially if work was something which could be shared.

In Figure 10d4 we have the person who is *interested in all humanity*, does not find it too easy to make it in such a close relationship as marriage, prefers the freer air of the group or society. They are happiest in detached relationships where the emotional demands are at a minimum. As companions they are great if your interests coincide.

Then we have the *short Heart line* (Figure 10d5) which only goes to under the Saturn mount. These people can be very sexy and charming when you first know them, but they tend to be selfish and changeful in love so for the person who is looking for the ideal and for the person with integrity this match would be nothing but a mismatch and a disaster. With both sexes there is a tendency to move swiftly from encounter to encounter once the initial stimulus and interest has died down. Where the line is lower there is more chance of a relationship continuing provided the partner is of the same 'ilk', that is also has a short Heart line finishing under the Saturn finger.

On the whole the shape, position, length and whether the Heart line has branches or not should really be matched by the partner's Heart line. The idealist matching the idealist, although the person who likes a peaceful haven at home will also find an affinity with the idealist. Those who put work first should either not marry or should marry another of their own kind; they will then understand each other's needs.

It is doubtful whether the short Heart line type ever finds happiness over a long period of time, as they are always searching on the principle that it is more blessed to travel hopefully than to arrive.

Where the *Heart line has three branches*, incorporating all those we have already discussed (Figure 10d), then we have to say that this person can be moody and changeable, up one moment, down the next, but never excessively so. If you like someone unpredictable and yet always stimulating, someone with this marking might be just your cup of tea.

Generally, if you look at the palms you will see two horizontal lines, the upper one of which is the *Heart line*, which we have been discussing, the lower the *Head line*, which we shall deal with later. Sometimes you will find there is just *one horizontal line* across the hand (Figure 10e) and this is called the *Simian* line, which stands in for both heart and head, which are fused in the nature giving a great deal of intensity, much concentration, and determination to achieve whatever goal the person has set – if it's you, you haven't got a hope of escaping, you've met your Fate, at least for the moment. You will find that the owner of the Simian line was much influenced by his/her mother who had definite plans for the child and very much dominated his/her psyche during the formative years.

Time and again I have found that the owner of the Simian line comes to grief in love. The reason for this is that, up to the age of 35 at least, the possessor of this line is jealous and insecure, so usually brings about the very thing he dreads, i.e. the loss of the loved object. After the age of 35 the doubts and insecurities of youth can be managed more easily where the person has a position and a family, and sees himself a little more confidently.

Where this Simian line exists in both hands you really do have a problem on your hands, for this type is intense not only about his love life, but also about his work. Fortunately, again after 35, he will achieve at least some of his ambitions, and so, while not exactly the most harmonious person to live with, he won't be quite impossible, only almost. You know the old tale, you takes your choice . . ..

As mentioned earlier in relation to all the lines, the Heart line too should be clear, long, nicely curved and free of islands, chains or breaks, all of which really show times of physical or psychological ill health. Being human beings and not angels, the worst blows we suffer in life are generally emotional and the Heart line mirrors these traumas.

THE HEAD LINE

This is a most important line, for it shows how we think; it is the barometer of our intellectual processes, and if it is much longer and stronger than the Heart line (Figure 10f1) you can be sure that this person is guided too much by his intellect and that as a result his emotional life suffers. He needs to learn to express his feelings more and not rely so much on his intellect. This is clearly seen where the Head line cuts across the hand from the thumb side to the percussion. Here you have a very intellectual type indeed, but also someone geared more to practicality, business or science than to the arts or fantasy.

The further the Head line goes across the hand, finishing perhaps under the Mercury mount then the capacity for abstract thought is present. If it is straight, but short, and goes only to an ending under the Saturn mount (Figure 10f2), you have a fairly earthy and commonsense personality. Flights of fancy or excursions into the abstract are not for him.

Where the Head line curves gently downwards (Figure 10f3) then you have the more imaginative, creative and artistic person. If it flows down too low as in Figure 10f4 then the imagination can be a problem; it can be too easy to escape into beautiful dreams away from this hard material world, especially if the rest of the hand is rather impractical too – with long fingers and long palm. Can you live with a dreamer? You might end up shouldering all the responsibilities of bread-winning, or bringing up the family or, worst of all, both.

Sometimes you see a Head line which trots along nice and straight for a while then takes a turn down the palm (Figure 10f5). This gives the best of all worlds, a combination of practicality and creativity, surely a signal of success.

The Simian line, mentioned earlier in connection with the Heart line, can of course also be considered in relation to the Head line, for it is the fusion of the two lines. We have to mention that it can be a regressive sign, as it is found in Down's Syndrome patients, but also in normal hands, where it bestows an intensity of concentration and the ability to compartmentalise the various areas of life and to apply energy exclusively and single-mindedly to the chosen subject or project. Simply because there is this capacity to concentrate with such intensity, it is unusual for such people to fail in their chosen subjects. Sometimes you will find that although a Simian line exists in a hand there are also branches coming from it either rising up or coming down (Figure 10e1); this gives more expression and allows the energy to be siphoned off, so to speak, making the person less obsessive.

Where and how the Head line starts is also relevant in relationships and compatibility in friendship or business associates. Look now at Figure 10g1 where the Head line starts in the Positive Mars mount. Here you have someone who can be a little defensive and touchy. Life was not easy in growing-up time and the child grew to thinking others were hostile. So this marks a touchy person.

In Figure 10g2, where the Head line continues to hug the Life line for anywhere up to an inch, then you have the very sensitive, dependent, family-oriented type, who leaves home late, the time marked by the time the line leaves the Life line. Family background and training are enduring influences throughout life. Although this person may never mention parents or early home life, nevertheless you must remember that there was a close attachment and this tendency to do as father or mother did will remain throughout life.

Where the Head line is separate from the Life line (Figure 10g3) in both hands you have a reckless, impulsive, self-confident type who will always tend to go their own way. This is of course the opposite to the tied Head line, where family teaching and a naturally cautious and careful nature can mean that progress is pretty slow in every way and happiness is likely to come late in life, as this type is a late developer.

Those of you who like to do things on the spur of the moment, like the open Head/Life line people, should steer clear of those whose Head and Life line hug one another. You would find it frustrating to be continually balked of action because . . . and you'd have to listen to all the reasons *why* you should not do such and such a thing.

Where the left or passive hand has a closed Head/Life line and the right or positive hand has an open one, you can safely note that the person has become more self-confident and has broken away from the family link.

Early difficulties within the family, or else health problems, can be marked by islands or little lines intermeshing the two lines of Head and Life so you'll know that you have some difficulties here to be talked and worked through if you really get together with this type in a loving way.

Again, it is much easier to get along with people who think as we do, have our own interests and hobbies and whose background is similar to our own, for then we don't have to understand another dimension; we simply understand because we were there, we were part of the same background – in fact our language is the same. Therefore, as you both examine your Head lines, remember that if they are different you have to make allowances and so learn to understand one another.

THE LIFE LINE

While we can say that the Heart and Head lines refer to our emotional and mental life respectively, the Life line (Figure 10h) refers to our actual living vitality, enjoyment of life and enthusiasm. As it's hard to enjoy one's life completely unless one is fit, the Life line also refers to our physical fitness and shows times when we are fit, enthusiastic and happy and other times when our health is down, or some accident or illness comes our way.

An old rather popular fallacy is that the Life line refers to the length of life we shall enjoy, and a favourite question levelled at hand-readers is 'and how long shall I live?' You have to explain that the Life line measures the quality of life, the health and happiness enjoyed by the person and not the length of time he will inhabit this planet.

To mention another popular fallacy which really does fill some people with dread if they see the mark of a broken Life line in their own or their loved ones' hands. It is because they think that either a short or a broken Life line advises them of their imminent demise. This is not so; remember that the lines can change and the short Life line is likely to grow, and is often found on young people's hands. The broken Life line refers to a complete change of life style, often of country even.

Situation

The Life line begins on the edge of the palm between the base of the thumb and the forefinger. If the line sweeps out into the hand (Figure 10h2) then the constitution is fine and robust, the stamina is excellent and the person likes plenty of activity; if the base of the palm is strong and heavy, especially with a practical or spatulate hand, then sport is much favoured. If as in Figure 10h1 the line tends to hug the mount of Venus, these people are not strong, not outgoing, rather reserved and cool in temperament. They reserve what physical energies they have for themselves so tend to be self-absorbed rather than outgoing.

The starting point

The interpretation of this is the same as we already mentioned for the Head line. Where the line is tied to the Head line then you have the cautious, careful type who thinks before he acts. The opposite is true where the lines are wide open at the beginning on both hands. If the right hand has an open formation and the left a closed one then the person often acts on impulse (the right-hand formation) and regrets at leisure (the left hand).

Endings

These tell us quite a bit about a person. If the Life line swings outwards as in Figure 10i1 towards the Luna mount, then the person looks to the freedom of travel and the wide open spaces, both physically and mentally. They have an enquiring, adventurous spirit.

If as in Figure 10i2 the Life line tucks back under the Venus mount you have someone who is home-loving and patriotic, not at all interested in foreign travel or adventure.

If as in Figure 10i3 there are two prongs, one tucking back and the other sailing off to the mount of Luna, then you have to decide which of these is stronger. Actually the person has a problem marked by the need to take a decision at the point where the line divides.

Sometimes the two hands have different endings. Often the passive hand only has a sweeping line out to Luna, while the active hand has a line which tucks under the Venus mount. This may mark frustration and disappointment since the partner may well not agree to emigration, or even to going back to one's roots at the end of life.

There are other indications of movement shown by branches dropping down off the Life line, the larger lines showing more important moves, the smaller ones a residential move.

So far as compatibility is concerned, it would seem wise for those with similar Life lines to get together; but more doubtful for those with dissimilar Life lines, whose starting point and ending were really dissimilar, unless other more important factors prevailed, to bring the likelihood of harmony.

9 The Fate, Sun and Other Lines

THE FATE LINE

If you want to know if your intended is going to be a success, or, put differently, feel happy and fulfilled careerwise, then you need to look at the Fate line. This line, situated in the centre of the palm, gives information about the 'public you'.

Beginnings

As we start this new chapter on the influence of lines I hope that our friends are still using the same method of study; of being together, but ideally situated across a small table, that you are both keeping your own little notebook containing any interesting bits of information you have come across to date.

The beginnings of the Fate line can differ, although the route it takes up the palm towards the Saturn finger is the same. Some Fate lines start on the *Luna mount* (Figure 11a1), and for these people fulfilment means being in the public eye, the entertainment world, as a performer, as a writer or singer or any other career which brings with it public acclaim.

There are Fate lines which start from the *Life line* (Figure 11a2); here there is attachment to the family and family responsibility keeps the child from going out into the great world to earn its living. When the line leaves the Life line, the child is free to fly the nest.

There are Fate lines which go *straight up the hand;* here is someone who works hard, saves his money and may stay in the same job for a life time. This particular pattern is not seen so much now. Its basic meaning is 'I assume my responsibilities for they are my fate'. The person with this deeply-cut straight Fate line (Figure 11a3) is a fatalist anyway!

If the Fate line *does not begin until further up the palm* (Figure 11b1), the person does not find his true career, his sense of purpose, until it does appear, although he may travel around a lot, do quite well prior to its appearance. Responsibility and a sense of control over his life does not appear until that magic time when the Fate line appears. With some people this does not happen until the age of 29–30 or, even later, 35, when marriage takes place and there is a need for a whole new outlook on life. Quite often I have been told that 'life was fun, but really purposeless until I met my wife, and then everything changed; I had to start to save to think of the future for us and for our children.'

Figure 11

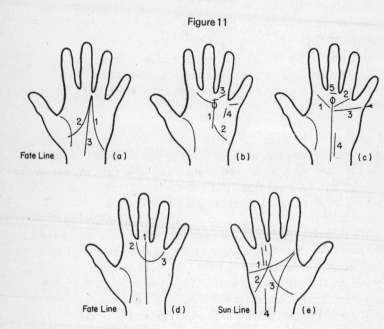

Where there are breaks or deviations in the line, there are changes in the career and changes in the way the person thinks about themselves in relation to their career.

When a line *enters the Fate line from the right* (Figure 11b2), this generally shows the advent of a new relationship which will develop into marriage or a permanant relationship. How the person's life is affected by the relationship is shown by the state of the Fate line *after* the line of Influence comes in from the mount of Luna. If it continues on strongly, then the marriage can be said to be a success. If, however, the *Influence line from Luna never joins the Fate line*, or cuts right through it, we can say this won't work at all, can even have a destructive effect. The same might be said if after the linking of the new line into the Fate line there was an island or bars cutting it (Figure 11b3).

If, however, there is a *complete break in the Fate line* after the entry of the Influence line, and a new line starts a little more to the right of the old line, this new section will represent a whole new, more successful life beginning (Figure 11b4).

I once had to do a radio spot for BBC Scotland and a whole bunch of handprints were sent to me for analysis, mostly unreadable; however, I do remember one which was unusual in that there were branches rising up to every finger from the Fate line (Figure 11c).

A branch up to the *Jupiter mount* (Figure 11c1) would signify some form of public recognition; this could have to do with politics, the Law, the Church or even higher educational successes, although the latter usually show up coming off the top of the Life/Head lines at about 19–21.

A branch up to the *Saturn mount* could not occur as the Fate line normally ends there anyway.

A branch up to the *Apollo or Sun mount* (Figure 11c2) would bring a focus to artistic or creative work and possible success in this line.

A branch up to the *Mercury mount* (Figure 11c3) would stress success in terms of scientific, commercial or business affairs.

Someone like the person whose hands I was asked to read was obviously someone who had a finger in many pies or, put more artistically, a jewel with many facets . . ..

It sometimes happens that the right hand, which is our outward-going or positive hand, shows a line from the Luna mount running up parallel with the Fate line; this generally shows an excellent business partnership, sometimes within a marriage (Figure 11c4).

There are set-backs in everyone's life, and these are marked on the Fate line as islands. The problem may be uncertainty due to lack of financial backing or fears over unemployment. Cuts in the line, where little bars cross it again show difficulties of various kinds (Figure 11c5).

If the *Fate line stops at the Head line* the traditional reading for this is that there has been a misjudgement which has adversely affected the career.

If the *Fate line stops at the Heart line*, again the traditional reading is that emotional entanglements cause career difficulties.

Endings
While it is usual for the Fate or Saturn line to end on the Saturn mount under the middle finger (Figure 11d1) it sometimes happens that the line veers over

to the Jupiter mount, showing personal success and public approbation (Figure 11d2). Another ending is under the Apollo or Sun finger (Figure 11d3); this shows success in creative, artistic work as a career.

So with viewing the Fate line you can see at least some part of your friend's past, present and future career and fortunes good or bad.

THE SUN LINE

When the Sun shines, most of us are happy, and the people who possess a Sun line are generally happy and fulfilled in a creative sense. In fact, pleased with the way in which their lives are working out, even if they are not positively involved in a creative way. They are generally warm, sunny, outgoing people who know what they like and are happy with it.

When the Sun line starts at the Heart line (Figure 11e1) you can be sure the person is going to have an emotionally and financially secure old age. An old saying relates that where there are three lines above the Heart line, there will be no want.

Sometimes the Sun line starts from the mount of Luna (Figure 11e2) and suggests success through the media, or some other way of attracting success through publicity. The earlier the Sun line starts the more cushioned the life in terms of money and the good things of life. In fact, if the Sun line starts from inside the Life line (Figure 11e3) then the parents were able to help gain success and financial stability for the person.

Very seldom you'll find a Sun line starting at the wrist or just above it (Figure 11e4); this signals very early stardom in some field much appreciated by the public.

It is to be noted that where the Sun line is absent, although the person may be most successful in the eyes of the world, their own perfectionist streak does not allow them to feel happy about their performance, and the Sun line does not exist in these hands. I have had to study the hands of many film and television artists and quite a few of them were without Sun lines.

So look to see when emotional and financial security comes your or your friend's way from finding the Sun line in the hand.

MINOR LINES

The Mercury line

This is a line which runs up towards the Mercury mount (Figure 12a), and is traditionally called the Hepatica, linking it with the health of our liver.

There used to be a saying that we are as old as the functioning of our arteries and our liver. It seems pretty certain that if we are not 100 per cent our judgement could be faulty and our business could suffer.

Figure 12

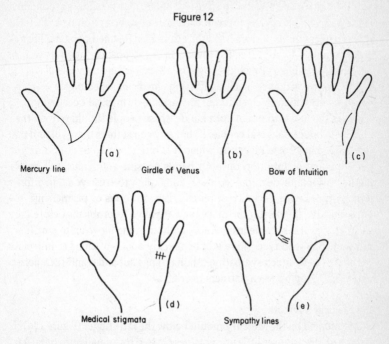

The line generally starts around the mount of Venus or the Life line and proceeds up to the Mercury mount. Breaks or a lot of little lines imply digestive difficulties.

Traditionally we are told that the only good Mercury line is the one that isn't there. However, experience suggests that a good clear line allows one to live fairly successfully.

The Girdle of Venus

This is a semi-circular line running under the fingers and above the Heart line (Figure 12b). It used to be considered a mark of sensuality and depravity, but on closer acquaintance through experience I find it endows the person with a great deal of sensitivity, and he or she is easily hurt emotionally. If the Girdle is broken up the hypersensitivity is tempered by a touch of realism.

The Bow of Intuition

Another semi-circular line, but this time on the percussion side of the hand; generally when fully marked the line runs from the Luna mount to the Mercury mount (Figure 12c). Where this line is present you have someone who is intuitive and sensitively alive and aware of atmosphere around her. These people possess the power of extra-sensory perception or ESP. If the bow is present in the passive hand the gift is used for their personal life and appreciation of family, friends, lovers. If in the positive hand as well or instead of, then it is a gift which is used in the career, and very useful it is too in any 'caring' situation such as nursing, medicine, mediumship; it also heightens insight and perception in any artistic or musical occupation.

Where the line is found in both hands, these people should rely on their 'hunches' about things and people. If they go against them they will find that they have made some mistakes, which it is often hard to undo. So, if you have this line of Intuition on both hands consult your inner self before making any major decision; you will come then to trust your own inner voice at times when a choice of paths arises. In terms of partnership, the more sensitive the person the more they are alive to problems before they grow, fester, and become insuperable without some blow-up to sort them out. Someone who is sensitive will be quickly aware of changes in feeling and atmosphere; quick sympathy, talking things out and comfort can often restore harmony between partners or friends.

The Medical Stigmata

This is situated on the Mercury mount below the little finger (Figure 12d). It consists of at least three little upright lines crossed by a small horizontal bar. The people who have this marking are really the most kindly and helpful types; they are ideally suited to working in the medical or veterinary field as they are specially gifted, being able to bring a soothing, calming atmosphere to any situation. Those who have this gift do not always become doctors, nurses or vets, but they do often gravitate into the growing field of alternative medicine. Although people who do not possess this little mark do go into medicine or a similar career, they are never as gifted as the person with the Medical Stigmata.

In this respect, I remember being consulted by a gentleman who was having problems in his love life. At the end of the consultation he said, 'You were not right about my career; I am not an engineer, I am a doctor.' This man had no Medical Stigmata, but he did have a very strong Fate line forging its way determinedly up the hand. I remember thinking at the time that his motivation careerwise was mainly financial and that his concern for his patients would always take second place.

If you marry someone with a Medical Stigmata you can be sure that whether they are professionally involved or not in the 'caring' field they will care for you, the family, the dogs, the cats and any other appendages or responsibilities you or yours have come to regard as your own.

You'll be even luckier if your partner has little oblique lines under the index finger as well as the Stigmata; you will have chosen well if it's someone to love and care for you and yours you were seeking. These lines are known as *Sympathy lines* (see Figure 12e).

Figure 13

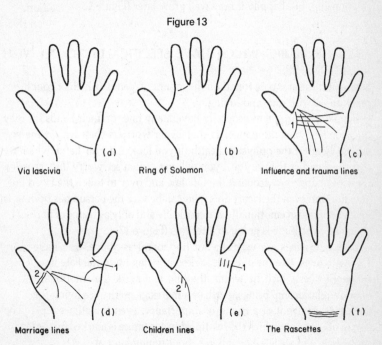

Via lascivia   (a)

Ring of Solomon   (b)

Influence and trauma lines   (c)

Marriage lines   (d)

Children lines   (e)

The Rascettes   (f)

The Via Lascivia

This is situated at the base of the Luna mount and is often semi-circular in shape (see Figure 13a). While the Girdle of Venus shows emotional vulnerability and sensitivity in that respect, the Via Lascivia suggests sensitivity in a physically responsive way. That is, the person who sports one of these is likely to be allergic to some substances such as drink, certain drugs, medicines, or just certain food allergies.

Traditionally, this line had as bad a name as the Girdle of Venus, suggesting all sorts of depravities; however, it does show sensitivity to poisons of all kinds and so danger to those addicted to alcohol or tobacco. If your friend or partner has this line or you have it yourself, take extra care with your diet.

The Ring of Solomon
Good judgement, maturity and wisdom are all marked by this semi-circular ring around the index finger. As this is gained through experience, if you and friend are young it is a mark you are not likely to find at the start of your relationship, but happily it may well grow later (Figure 13b).

LINES OR MARKS WHICH HAVE SPECIFICALLY TO DO WITH RELATIONSHIPS
Many of these are to be found on the mount of Venus, which of course has much to do with love and loving.

People with problems generally have many lines on their hands for they are worriers, and the danger is that being worriers they will in the end adversely affect their physical health. If you look at a 'Full' hand, which we described earlier (Figure 10b), you will very often see worry lines crossing the mount and even crossing the Life line and over to touch the Head line, Fate line and even the Heart line. You can be sure the person has been or is given to living an emotionally traumatic life and only a change of partner or a change of attitude is going to alter this (Figure 13c).

Where the lines are vertical, not horizontal as above, you have more Influence lines, like the ones we looked at rising up to the Fate line. These Influence lines which lie within the Life line mark the emotional charge which a relationship brings, perhaps a marriage, perhaps a living-together, perhaps the advent of a friend of importance, even sometimes a pet. The length of time over which the relationship continues is marked by the length of the line, and we shall be talking about timing later on.

Traditionally the so-called *Marriage lines*, little horizontal lines running on the upper percussion under the Mercury finger (Figure 13d1), were said to show the number of marriages and their relative length and timing. This is sometimes so, but sometimes it simply doesn't work at all; for instance two bachelors well set into middle life, who are unlikely to marry, have wonderfully strong marriage lines.

Often we can give a double check on the small *Family ring* encircling the

92

base of the thumb, for this ring will often tell of marriage, divorce or bereavement. Sometimes you will find the Family ring is broken into two which suggests a broken marriage. Sometimes there will be two Family rings; the possibility of there being two marriages is then present (Figure 13d2).

You can check then your findings on the percussion, whose timing is pretty limiting owing to the whole of the life having to be contained within the space of about an inch between the Heart line and the base of the Mercury finger. The lower the line the earlier the attraction, midway is about the 40 mark, then 60 and so on up to the base of the Mercury finger.

Children lines are little vertical lines which drop down onto the Marriage lines on the Mercury mount (Figure 13e1). It is said that the thick ones represent boys and the thin ones girls. However, you must also be aware that many people have lots and lots of tiny lines above their Marriage line. Somehow I don't think that in this day and age people would be too anxious to bring up all the children which God in his mercy seems to have promised some via their hand markings. This really tells you a) this person is fond of children; b) this person who is fond of children may well work with them, teach them – look after them in a nursery, may be a children's nurse; c) the children may be her sisters' and she is particularly fond of them. So, you see, you cannot take these markings too literally at times.

Marriage lines on the mount which *split* often refer to partners who have different interests, stay together, but go their own ways socially, or in terms of hobbies and interests. Sometimes the split marks divorce. When the *Marriage line* drops down to the Heart line traditional teaching forecasts bereavement.

As Influence lines are shown within the Life line as vertical lines so the advent of a child is shown by tiny lines or branches which drop down inside the Life line (Figure 13e2).

Incidentally, the *Family ring* encircling the base of the thumb is not only to be taken as an indicator of marriage or relationship, but also often marks the beginning of family problems with a line running over the Venus mount and even crossing the Life line when the problem comes out into the open and people outside the family get to know about it (Figure 13c1).

While the *Rascettes*, which are often known as the Bracelets, and are situated on the uppermost part of the wrist abutting onto the palm (Figure 13f), are not so directly related to compatibility and relationships as the lines and marks we have just been considering, they do have a bearing on health.

Traditionally, the Bracelets were considered to have a bearing on health, wealth and happiness. If the first three Rascettes were well-formed, then the lucky owner was considered to have a healthy, wealthy and happy life before him or her. If an additional Rascette was present, bringing the number up to four, then the person was also promised longevity.

Modern palmists are neither so full of Fire and Brimstone in their warnings, nor as wholly cheerful, encouraging, and marvellously optimistic in their positive pronouncements as their predecessors, but perhaps this merely reflects the various shades of grey which constitute modern life, nothing really being either black or white any more.

What we can say about the Rascettes is that if the first Rascette rises up into the palm, then if the client is a lady she will have gynaecological problems; if a man the likelihood is of urological difficulties.

My dear friends, I do hope you have found this chapter informative too, and that you will now have a nice break and consider your findings – probably have a good laugh to balance with laughter the serious concentration necessary.

10 Timing of Events, General Assessment and Romance

To my two friends I would say that you must have learnt a great deal up to now, and some of it you'll have in your memory box and some in your notebooks. Of course the more 'telling' the titbit about your friend the easier you will find recall, and the same will apply to their memory bank. Perhaps one of you has said that it would be nice to know how to time things on the hand and this is exactly what we are going to do now.

There are many systems of timing which have been put forward by various well-known palmists, but I think that every practising palmist evolves a system which works for them, a system which is evolved by experience. If you are not too sure when you first start looking at hands, try and find some important event on the hand you are reading and establish the time of this event. You will then be able to work backwards or forwards in time, hopefully with more success as you become more used to the system. At present of course we are just trying to give you some guidelines which you can use yourself to date events in your own and your partner's hands.

Note too that, although palmistry or the science/art of hand-reading is such a maddeningly fascinating subject, bringing so much interesting information the way of the student, where time is concerned you do not have the exactitude of the astrological chart drawn up for the exact time, date and place of birth. You cannot pinpoint an event to the month, week or day of occurrence, but it is worthwhile to have some prior notification up to six months or a year when such an event might be happening.

Most palmists find by a process of trial and error the system which suits them best; it will be one which is correct for them for the various hand sizes and shapes which arrive for their perusal, but the most commonly-used system is Cheiro's count of 7. The hand is marked off in 7-year periods; the years in between can be counted as dots, one dot per year. It is probable that Cheiro chose 7 as the body is said to renew itself entirely every 7 years.

TIMING ON THE LIFE LINE

If you look at Figure 14 you will see how to read time on the Life line. The line is marked from the top of the Life line from 7 to 77 and beyond. A dot with the pen for a year's span makes a convenient and generally accurate assessment. Remember though that you must adjust your measurements to the size of the hand; obviously you're going to be more pushed for space on a small hand than you are on a large, masculine hand. Here you can afford to be a bit more expansive.

Figure 14

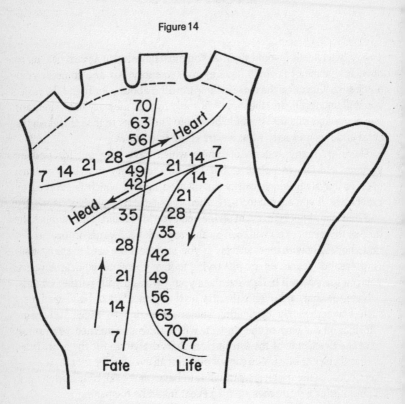

TIMING ON THE FATE LINE

Most hand readers reckon 35 coincides with the client's Head line, although I have seen some who mark it at 40 or even 45. You time on the Fate line just as you have done on the Life line, but moving upwards from the base of the hand.

TIMING ON THE HEAD LINE

Although many palmists consider it is not possible, or rather not effective, to date on the Head line, it is something which is quite easy once you have established your guidelines. Again follow the system of 7, moving from the 7 mark at the beginning of the line and following the arrow. In taking your measurements try to establish with your friend the date of some event of meaning; you can then work backwards and forwards from this point.

You will find that if you drop a line with your pen or pencil from the base of the middle of the Saturn finger to the Life line, this point will mark on the Life line about 40 or roughly the middle of your subject's life. If you are pushed for time or you want to make a check on your markings this is a good tip to remember. If you were working from a print the same procedure would apply, but this is something we are not going to involve ourselves in at the moment as this is intended as a personal handbook for lovers and friends.

However, I will include a 'how to do it', that is how to take outlines and prints, at the end of the book for those who'd like to try.

TIMING ON THE HEART LINE

Probably fewer people use the Heart line for timing than use the Head line, but it is perfectly possible to do so and to get good results. Since, to my way of thinking, the Heart line starts on the percussion under the edge of the Mercury finger, I have tabulated it in this way. However, there are those who think that it starts under the Jupiter or even Saturn fingers, or wherever to me it ends; if you agree, then you must of course reverse your reading, starting with 7 under the Jupiter or Saturn finger. However, it really does seem to complicate matters for those of you who are just starting to get acquainted with hand-reading, so probably you'd better stick with the text and you will find your results are effective.

GENERAL ASSESSMENT OF OTHER PEOPLE

Up till now we have been considering just the two of you, but we cannot always be together with those we love, so it might be helpful to have a quick look at those we meet every day, our fellow workers, associates and those in authority.

You may find this exercise both tantalising and frustrating, tantalising because you can only see so much and frustrating because you can't see more without being thought a bit odd. So, although you may have to operate rather surreptitiously, gradually you will build up a picture of those you see every day in the course of your work. Your findings may confirm or contradict your assessment of your work mates, which you had already made before you became interested in Palmistry. You'll be able to see the shape of the hands and fingers as well as the thumb. You'll probably find you have to leave examination of the lines to those of family and friends who are interested enough to allow you to examine their hands in more detail.

We have gone into the hand shapes quite deeply earlier, and so you will know the compatibility and whether you are going to get on in a general sense with your new boss or colleague.

Compare the finger type; long or short, fat or thin, knuckled or smooth? Also, especially where the new boss is concerned, is the thumb shapely, tough-looking or is the top joint heavy? If the latter, watch out for explosions!

OUR ROMANTIC LIFE

A quick recap here may be of use. First of all look to the *hand* and *finger* contrasts and compatibilities when it is love which occupies our mind. This, if you remember, is always basic and so important.

Having done this we need to compare the lines of Heart, most important where lovers are concerned, and the lines of Head. The latter because the way we think shapes who we are, whether we are extroverted, introverted, critical, easy-going, intellectual or non-academic. The rational, reasonable types will be shown by the straight Head line, the imaginative creative ones by the curving down Head lines, and the very sloping Head lines can be moody and over-imaginative.

Finally, the question which is foremost in many people's mind is 'Will I marry and if so when?' Now, these are things which you who have been following these chapters carefully know you can answer, even the timing question 'When?'

In Palmistry, as you will know now, Influence lines are very important as they actually do refer to a person, someone who will influence your life for good or ill.

Remember where you will find the first Influence lines. Look at Figure 15a where you will see them in relation to the Fate line. These can be seen very clearly in the hand. In Figure 15a1 you will see an Influence line entering the

Fate line; this means someone comes into your life, and, if after the arrival of this someone the Fate line develops an island or is crossed by a bar or bars, then there are problems in the relationship.

Figure 15

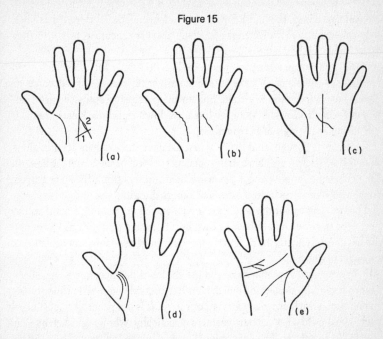

Look now at Figure 15a2. Here we have an Influence line which appears at first to be in great difficulty, with a crossing bar showing family opposition and an island showing doubt and uncertainty. However, you'll see it improves and reaches the Fate line, thus giving stability to the relationship, maybe marriage, and if the Fate line strengthens after then all will be well.

In Figure 15b we have a line which never reaches the Fate line, a factor which can show agonising delay for the parties, although of course caused by one. The relationship never stabilises and becomes a real union.

In Figure 15c you'll see that the *Influence* line cuts through the Fate line, and this spells disaster – the marriage never takes place, or the relationship never stabilises.

Remember to gauge the effect of the relationship on the subject by the look of the Fate line after the union.

Then remember the *Influence* lines inside the Life line (Figure 15d); if these

99

continue to follow the Life line then all is well with the relationship, but if the line begins to veer off towards the ball of the thumb the marriage is failing.

Other signs are the *Marriage* lines on the percussion under the Mercury finger. These are not always very accurate, but they are traditionally, with the Influence lines, the signs of marriage. Sometimes the Children lines, little vertical lines above the Marriage lines, are also very accurate, but often they reflect a person's love of children.

The *Family ring*, which has much to do with family fortunes, also often symbolises marriage. Breaks in the Family ring can signify divorce or separation. Where the Marriage line on the percussion splits (Figure 15e), divorce often follows. Where the line dips down to hit the Heart line, it is traditionally the sign of bereavement.

Remember, though, that firstly you must never take one indication alone in making a judgement, and, in the particular aspect of the Marriage lines on the percussion, some people swear by them, others think they are correct some of the time, as indeed I do, and others disdain them altogether.

You are reading for the whole person when you are reading a hand and so you need to relax and allow your own intuitions and perceptions to operate as well as applying the basic tenets you read about here or in any other book on hand reading.

In Western society, marriage and the choice of partners has always been seen as a gamble, something which is entirely outside the usual rational rules of conduct, which normally govern our lives. It is not generally questioned that we should choose our partners practically wholly guided by our emotional reactions. This is a way of conduct which is accepted as valid by our society. The result has been an epidemic of divorces. I think statistics show that one in four marriages in England end in the divorce court. We now have a new phenomenon, the single-parent family.

In India marriage is considered as being a very important matter, not only to the two people most closely concerned, but also to their families. Generally, it is the parents who seek a suitable mate for their son or daughter aided by the astrologer who will draw up the natal charts of any proposed suitors. In this way it is possible to see whether any two people are suitable partners, whether they will like the same things, will both agree on children and of course be of the same religious as well as ethnic background. Today this way of dealing with marriage, which has been proven to be much more successful than the haphazard Western way of doing things, is being eroded, where the younger Indian folk wish to follow the ways of their Western friends and pick their partners as they will.

No doubt the result of this gradual erosion of the old values will bring a similar result to the Western one. We have to remember too that, until recently, say about 20–30 years ago, parents in the Western world had much more say in their children's choice of partner and irate Victorian-style fathers could refuse to give their daughter's hand in marriage to a man of whom they did not approve.

This is all leading up to the suggestion that much unhappiness could be avoided if before marriage a little more could be known about the compatibility of the proposed partners on every level, mental, emotional, physical and sexual. I have suggested that you work as two friends who are out to understand themselves and one another better, and that if possible you keep a notebook of the important findings. This will help you not to walk blindfold into what might well be a disaster, but to be able to assess the areas of possible stress and struggle. You can then, both of you, decide whether you reckon it is all worth taking a chance on your being able to cope with these differences of opinion or not.

The trouble is that we are all, when young especially, driven by our instincts and the physical attraction of guys or girls. This is not enough to hold a marriage or permanent relationship together; you can't stay in bed all your life . . . ..

As we have seen in past chapters, the hand reveals the truth about a person and will tell you the important things you need to know before entering into a lifelong partnership. In going through the book carefully you'll gain a working knowledge of Palmistry which will stand you in good stead now and in the future. For some of you it may mean the start of a new hobby, which you can practise on your family and friends to gain expertise.

Talking of families, many of you will be looking at the hands of members of your family. They are so to speak convenient victims. You love them and are interested in them, so it is a good case for examining their hands closer.

Just as an astrological birthchart drawn up and interpreted for the date, time and place of a person's birth will show many planets in similar signs, positions or angles as older members of the family, a sort of family signature that is passed on from generation to generation, resulting in similar characteristics repeating themselves within the family, so various indications in the hand are also repeated from generation to generation. This gives what we might call the family hand signature. You can see this clearly, particularly if you have three generations hands before you for your interpretation.

Sometimes it is the hand shape which is similar, sometimes it is the digit length, breadth and shape, sometimes it is the Heart or Head lines which are similar. You can tell then, even when the child is quite young, for the major lines are formed early on in the womb, whether a child is going to be like father, mother, grandmother or grandpapa, and this also explains a seeming mystery of why some family members get along so much better than others; the reason is, of course, that they have similar characteristics, which can be seen in the hand shape, the fingers, the mounts and the lines.

We mentioned that, when comparing the hands of lovers, one of the most important lines to look at was the Heart line, for, while the whole hand will tell you about the whole person, the Heart line will give a quick report of how a person responds and reacts emotionally. In the family, then, where the Heart lines are similar they will share and understand their feelings, be able to sympathise easily with one another. This is very important between a mother and her child, also between father and child, as this understanding will help in the child's upbringing.

When dealing with colleagues and friends it was mentioned that similar Head lines were a flash-point for understanding one another, for it shows a similar way of thinking, similar likes and dislikes, an intellectual understanding. Where the Head lines are similar in family members, you will get interests in common and a generally similar way of looking at life.

It is differences in ways of looking at life both intellectually and emotionally which makes the home a happy place, or a place of continual bickering and sometimes bitter feuding, which sometimes continues even when the parties have grown up and left home.

When you are examining hands, perhaps even you two friends may find this so. You find one hand is different from the other, not too often in shape, although the fingertips may vary, but very often in terms of lines. Here you have a case of the child inheriting characteristics from both parents. If the parents were in harmony, the child will not have too many difficulties, but will exhibit different attitudes and reactions from time to time. If the left or passive hand is like mother's, the child will have similar emotional responses to life as his mother. If the positive or right hand is like father's, he will appear to the world to be very like his father, for the right or positive hand is like the mask which we wear to greet the world where we wish, of course, to appear in the best possible light.

So if you wish to gain a working knowledge of Palmistry and also gain some further knowledge and understanding of your family, make as careful an examination of the hands as you can and may you all find both enjoyment and insight.

11 Fingernails, Fingerprints and Other Palmar Patterns

FINGERNAILS

Fingernails imply also fingertips, for the nails follow the shaping of the skin. Traditionally, it was considered that the life force entered the body through the fingertips and that the various shapes presented by the nails either allowed the force to flow in easily or presented some resistance to it, and this in turn imprinted certain characteristics upon the owners of the different nail shapes.

Your natural powers of observation will of course allow you to draw certain conclusions about a person's character just by a quick look at the way in which the nails are groomed. If the nails are neatly cut and filed you will assume the person is careful and fastidious in personal hygiene. If the nails are dirty and uncared for your assumptions will not be so charitable. If the nails are bitten you will assume the person is anxious and tense. The closer to the skin the nail is bitten the more self-destructive the person. The frustrations are likely to emerge during the hand-reading, and it may be possible to suggest ways of altering the life situation so that the anxieties and frustrations are reduced.

While the shape of the nails tells much about an individual's character and attitudes to life, it is first and foremost a health indicator, and therefore we shall be dealing with nails in this context in a later chapter. An examination of them for a health check would be more difficult if the nails are painted according to fashion, as many indications would be missing.

Although nails can be divided into a number of categories, the most basic and necessary ones will be given here with their descriptive qualities.

Figure 16a refers to people with large square nails. These people are easy-going and generally placid unless roused. The attitude is painstaking, cautious and workmanlike. Anything attempted is done with skill and attention to detail.

Figure 16b refers to people with small square nails. These people tend to be rather critical and narrow-minded in outlook.

Figure 16c shows the wide square nail, broader than it is long. These people have the breadth of outlook denied to the small square nail, but they have an explosive temper, which once it is over is quickly forgotten and everything proceeds as before. However, you have to possess strong nerves to cope with this type in close relationship.

Figure 16

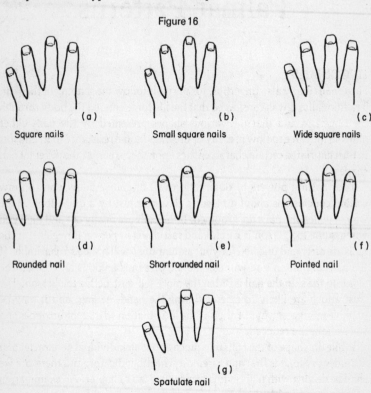

(a)
Square nails

(b)
Small square nails

(c)
Wide square nails

(d)
Rounded nail

(e)
Short rounded nail

(f)
Pointed nail

(g)
Spatulate nail

Figure 16d shows a nice rounded nail, and these people are generally easy to get along with and good company; however, if upset they tend to hold their hurt inside and so sulk or go into a bout of silence.

Figure 16e shows the shorter version of the above; in this case the person is more impatient and so less tolerant in difficult situations.

Figure 16f is a pointed nail showing a sensitive, refined gentle type, often possessing good intuitive powers.

Figure 16g is the spatulate nail, which indicates that the owner of this shape of nail is essentially individualistic, good with their hands, and they can generally cope with anything which comes their way, as they are endowed with energy and intelligence.

Naturally, dear friends, when you are examining hands just add the knowledge you get from one part of the hand to the information you already have, look for confirmation or modification in other parts of the hand, or in your case from the notes you already have. Remember never to make a final judgement on one factor only. Build up your picture as you go along, rather like a painting which grows as the artist proceeds with the creation.

FINGERPRINT PATTERNS

Although the lines on the hands change as our ideas and lifestyles change, the fingerprint patterns are ones which never change from birth to death; we keep them because they are part of our genetic inheritance. I have heard that criminals anxious to avoid the deductions of the police fingerprint experts have tried to have their prints burned off with acid. Alas, this desperate ruse did not work, as even through the acid treatment the original fingerprint pattern still emerged.

It is also interesting to note that these patterns are also the last to disappear from the hands upon the death of the subject. A student of the Society in an excess of zeal was able to study this factor, as she had friends who had recently been bereaved and the body was to remain in the home until the date of the funeral. While the lines were gradually eroded after death the fingerprint patterns were the last to go.

These patterns then represent the individual's basic attitude to life and therefore are very important in assessing personality and reaction in a person-to-person situation.

An early pioneer in the study of fingerprints was Francis Galton, who collected and classified thousands of hand prints, thus proving their value in criminal identification. A later pioneer, Beryl Hutchinson, also did sterling work on identifying and classifying the various patterns, which are described in her book, *Your Life in Your Hands*.

There are *five basic patterns* which have important meanings in terms of perception and understanding, as well as being health indicators.

1) *The loop* (Figure 17a and b). These people are adaptable and easy-going. They like to work with others.

2) *The whorl* (Figure 17c). This indicates a great deal of fixity in the nature. The individualist.

3) *The arch* (Figure 17d). These also tend to be fixed people. Very practical and reliable.

4) *The composite* (Figure 17e). Entwined loops. Dualistic in approach to life.

5) *The tented arch* (Figure 17f). A sort of 'frozen' arch pattern. Idealists.

Figure 17

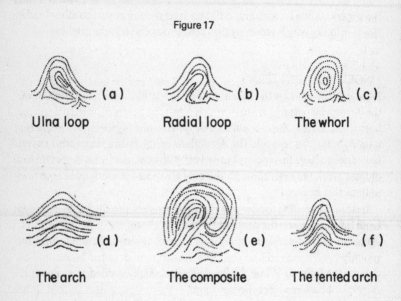

Ulna loop   Radial loop   The whorl

The arch   The composite   The tented arch

The loop pattern

This is very often present in two varieties. Whether one or the other, its presence endows the individual with a graceful adaptable personality with a love of change and variety. Plenty of challenge is required and a dull, repetitive life would not attract at all.

The two varieties are the ulna and the radial loop. The *ulna loop* (Figure 17a) is thrown towards the thumb side of the hand from the percussion. The *radial loop* (Figure 17b) is thrown or pointed towards the percussion from the thumb side of the hand.

Where the *ulna loop* is a dominant pattern in the hand then there is a cautious 'look and see first' attitude before jumping into or out of any situation. Where the *radial loop* is a dominant pattern in the hand these people are more inclined to make their own decisions, irrespective of the advice of others. They are more self-determining.

It is interesting to note that with the dominance of either loop patterns on the fingertips the individual readily accepts new ideas, they have open minds and rarely dismiss things out of hand. Psychologically, they are highly-strung and cannot stand too much tension over a long period of time.

The whorl

This is the mark of the individualist (Figure 17c) and is not so often found as the loop pattern. Miss Hutchinson states that about 25 per cent of all prints exhibit the whorl pattern.

Everything is extremely well thought out, and once decisions are made the whorl pattern individual does not change his mind. However, they are generally slow to respond and the attitudes and habits learnt in childhood and early life are rarely changed, hence the label often given as 'fixed'. They have, of course, the positive virtues of their natures. These are determination, persistence, strength and the ability to withstand great adversity. Loyal and firm, they can be relied upon to look after you and the family.

Being individualistic, they do not make good team-mates; they prefer to work for themselves and to be in charge.

People with a full set of whorls always aim to work for themselves and are rarely happy until they do.

Although a full set of whorls is rare, a whorl on the third finger is often found, in which case it indicates original creative or artistic ability. Often good cooks or designers, these people are most gifted. Never try to change their minds once they have made them up – they will accuse you of never knowing your own mind, of being changeable and vacillating, while they are models of virtue in knowing exactly what they want and going all out for it. This latter interpretation is particularly true if the thumb is a whorl pattern. In any case the whorl pattern individual is a complex type, very intense and often introverted.

The whorled little finger is never a superficial type, but once embarked on his favourite topic he'll ride his hobby horse to exhaustion – yours or his, and maybe both.

The problem with the whorl in relationships is *they care* and do so intensely, wherever their interests or yours are concerned. They can be totally callous where the interests of others with whom they have little in common are concerned. In fact, emotionally and in love, they are an all-or-nothing type.

The arch
The arch type digital pattern (Figure 17d) is indicative of a down-to-earth practical, reliable type of person. You know where you are with them; if they say they'll do a thing they'll do it as promised or there'll be a very good reason why they can't. They are very stable people, but often limited in their understanding and in their ambitions. On the whole they do not have a great deal of self-confidence and so often give up trying before they really should.

If you are attracted to someone whose dominant digital pattern is the arch, remember they find it difficult to express their feelings, and often repress them, and so suffer with strain and tension. This difficulty in expressing their emotions is specially acute when the forefinger and middle fingers are arched. If some practical creative or artistic outlet can be found for them, this will prevent too much repression with consequent mental or emotional distress.

Where the thumbs bear arched patterns you have trustworthy, down-to-earth people who can find that they are props to weaker brethren.

In relationships and work the arch types are tops for reliability, courage and coping. As they are down-to-earth types they prefer the conversation to stick with fairly mundane matters such as the price of beef this week or Mrs Brown's bad toe – flights of fancy are not in their line at all, nor abstract principles; they are happiest in *doing* and doing whatever it is well. They are very good at positive and constructive effort, especially if the thumbs bear this pattern. So, if it's reliability you are seeking, these people undoubtedly fill this bill.

The composite
This can be recognised by the fact that the pattern has entwined loops pulling in opposite directions (Figure 17e). It resembles the whorl in looks, but not in attitude. In fact the composite might be said to be the opposite; dualistic in attitude, these people are always seeing both sides of a problem or question, weighing and balancing the decisions carefully, generally ending up in total disarray, as either opportunity or choice which is being considered seems to come to the same thing the more the person considers it. With them their second name might be *indecision*, as they find it so difficult to make up their minds.

Traditionally, it is said to be a good pattern on the forefinger and thumb for those in the legal profession. Perhaps it is easier to make professional and objective decisions, where it still remains hard to be decisive in personal matters.

If you find it easy to make up your mind, you could find the composite type really irritating. However, they do need someone decisive as a partner.

The tented arch
This is an arch with a sort of 'tent pole' effect (Figure 17f), and its characteristics are totally different from the arch pure and simple, which we have just been discussing. These are the idealists who possess open minds and are always searching for solutions. They really need groups and societies through which they can work for their ideals. Keeping up their enthusiasm is very important to their happiness; they can work selflessly for their chosen ideal. They are highly-strung and often artistic or musical. They should not be subject to too much pressure as they often suffer with nerve problems. It is important for you, my dear friends, to weigh up and evaluate these basic characteristics.

Figure 18

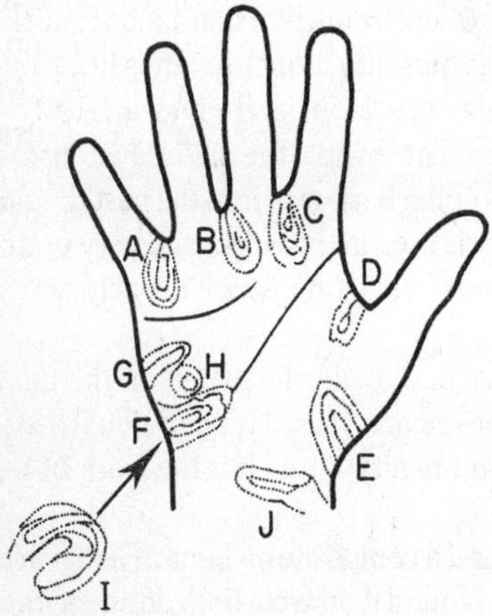

A. Humour
B. Serious intent
C. Executive ability
D. Courage
E. Music
F. Memory loop
G. Affinity with nature
H. Individualistic unconscious
I. Composite intuitive clarity
J. Inspiration

PALMAR PATTERNS
In Figure 18A we have a small loop between the little and the third or Sun finger. You know that this person possesses a good sense of humour, something very necessary in life and particularly in family life. A great asset.

In Figure 18B, between the Sun or third finger and the middle or Saturn finger, you will also find a small loop. This is called the 'loop of serious intent', showing the individual wants to make something of his life and would prefer to do something which helped someone else. This is often found on the hands of nurses or doctors.

The loop in Figure 18C, between the middle and the forefinger, is said to give executive ability; it is rarely seen and has been named the *Rajah loop*. Good of course for professional types.

In Figure 18D, found within the Venus/Mars Positive mount between the thumb and forefinger, we have a little *loop of courage*.

Figure 18E shows the loop on the mount of Venus. There are many little marks on this mount which refer to musical ability or musical appreciation, and a loop here on the mount will show at least appreciation if not the ability to perform.

Other Palmar patterns can also be found on the *mount of Luna* and the *Neptune mount*.

In Figure 18G the loop coming in here from the percussion on the Luna mount relates to an understanding of and affinity with nature; the person who has green fingers, whose plants rarely die. You'll also find dancers with this loop showing their affinity with nature in terms of rhythm.

The loop in Figure 18F usually comes up from the Luna mount on the percussion side, and the Head line either dips into it or else stands just short of doing so. This is known as the *Memory loop*, and gives a retentive memory to its owner. Found on the left hand, the individual has a marvellous memory for family matters going back well into the past. Found on the right hand, the retentive memory is used in the work, and very useful it is too, particularly in those professions like acting where the actor must memorise his lines.

As in Figure 18H you will sometimes find a whorl situated on the Luna mount, which is said to individualise the unconscious. This individual needs creative fulfilment in terms of helping humanity; often it is the mark of the natural healer or psychic.

As in Figure 18I sometimes you will find a composite on Luna. This is rare, but I have found it; and the two people I found it on were both dowsers, that is people who are skilled at finding water under the surface of the earth. They may of course look for other things, such as minerals or oil, but the two I knew used the pendulum in checking out their medical diagnoses and also used it to find the homeopathic remedies which should be given to their patients. People who work in this way are called radiesthetists, but the psychic ability is the same as the dowsers use.

The loop in Figure 18J which rises from the wrist and proceeds over the mount of Neptune is not very often found. It is said to show artistic ability and helps painters and poets to express themselves as it indicates a flow of inspiration from the unconscious. While the palmar patterns are not so basic and important in terms of characteristics, nevertheless they add a little more to your build-up of that most complex of animal/angels, the human being. The two who have been following this all along must have quite a full notebook and also lots in your memory bank by now, and I do hope you are enjoying it.

12 Health

The greatest gift that we can have is good health. Some people are born healthy; some have to achieve it with care and attention. The hand can be helpful in pointing out possible weaknesses, which with care can be prevented or their effects minimised. After all the hand cannot lie, it tells its own tale of good, bad, or indifferent health, but we need to be able to interpret the signs, and this is what we shall be aiming to do in this chapter.

It is always important to be able to detect an illness in its early stages so that swift action can make for a swift cure.

In earlier chapters we looked at the basic hand types, and therefore we can first of all consider the type of weaknesses which go with the hand shapes.

The Elementary type. This is rarely seen now in its pure form, but the subject's health is generally good, they thrive in the open air, and as they tend to be moody their health problems seem to come later in life in terms of depressive illness.

The Square and Oblong types. These are also generally healthy people, but particularly the Square tend to overwork and worry. This makes for stress, which in turn can lead to illness. The best advice to these two types is to have a nice break from time to time, even if this only means changing your work for a demanding hobby. It is the demanding hobby which will enable them to relax more than taking the traditional sunbathing and sitting toasting on the beach type of holiday.

The Spatulate type. Of all the basic types these are the most vital and energetic so it is probable that it is only burning the candle at both ends which will cause these individuals to let up and rest.

The Conic type. These are the people who can 'dig their graves with their teeth'. Towards middle life the Conic type tends to run to fat and endanger not only their beauty, but their health. To keep healthy Conic types need to moderate their appetites and so avoid too much sugar and carbohydrates.

The Psychic type. These are the most sensitive and impressionable of all the shapes. They do not have the high energy levels of some of the other types. Being less practical they often do not find coping with the material world an easy matter and can try escaping through drink or drugs, to which they are often also allergic. They need a kind, understanding partner, who is also practical and so able to cope with difficult decisions and daily living problems.

SKIN TEXTURE, COLOUR AND TEMPERATURE

Now, my two dear friends, at this point you need once again to be seated comfortably opposite one another to examine the hand. Where the skin is fine and soft there is, as mentioned above on the Psychic type, a sensitivity to the environment, the colds, germs and virus infections which often seem to be around. This skin type will also be more sensitive to various allergic conditions. Where the skin is tougher there is less sensitivity to the environment; if the skin is really dry and scaly, though, there may be a tendency towards an under-active thyroid, over-active if the hands are warm and wet.

The normal skin colour on the palm of the hand is a nice rosy pink showing good health and normal functioning of the body. If the skin is red there may be a tendency to high blood pressure, and it would be possible and helpful to ask whether this has been checked recently. A pale skin suggests a lack of energy which could be due to anaemia; this very often happens with women of child-bearing age. There are some good iron mixture tablets on the market, which could be of help. Where the skin shows up as yellow, your friend may have recently suffered from some liver complaint such as jaundice, or even a bilious attack can cause this temporarily.

If the hands feel cold, although the room temperature in which you are both sitting is warm, then there is poor circulation.

HEALTH AS SEEN IN THE HAND

As you pick up the hand it should be neither too soft nor too hard, it should feel warm to the touch and of a nice consistency. The nails should be free of ridges, either vertical or horizontal, a matter we'll deal with later in more detail. The nails should also have moons on all fingers and thumbs. The fingertips should not be crossed with lines. The lines on the hand should not be too numerous, nor crossed with random lines, islands and bars should be kept to the minimum. The Health line, if present at all, should be single and

114

unbroken; the Life line and indeed all the other lines on the hand should be strongly defined.

In the last ten years or so it has been brought into the public mind that *tension* is one of the main contributing factors in physical illness. It seems to be agreed that the ability to relax would help to reduce the stress which causes tensions, hence the growth of new movements; meditation, yoga, Tai-Chi, all of which aim to help the Westerner to 'let go' and 'let God', as I'm sure Billy Graham would say.

We mentioned earlier on that there were two main types, those with the *empty* hand and those with the *full* hand. It is the latter which gives evidence of stress. These people are born worriers, with nervous systems which react to the smallest problem. The nervous system is always on guard, a habit learnt in childhood probably, where the emotional security was most likely missing, never to be replaced later in life.

Exhaustion is often found by the dropping in of the skin on the fingertips accompanied by downward lines, which are generally curved to fit the drooping of the skin. Where you see this indication do just suggest the person eases up as soon as possible.

There are several other stress indications in the hand and another which has to do with the fingertips. Where you see lines running across the fingertips you can be sure there are unresolved problems causing tension in this person's life. The area of life which is causing the problem can be interpreted from the finger which has these little horizontal crossing lines. The more of these there are on any particular finger, the more the anxieties present in that area of life symbolised by the stressed fingertip.

If there are many lines on the forefinger then the problem relates to the person's ego and self-confidence. If on the Saturn or Middle finger the problems relate to security and career matters. If on the ring or Apollo finger, the problem relates either to fulfilment in love or in an artistic or creative sense. Where the little finger has these lines then the problem relates to sexual frustrations or difficulties or to self-expression in a literary or scientific way.

In practice, it's rarely easy to pinpoint the problem, except possibly finding the finger with the 'mostest', for it's likely that all the tips have some cross-markings in this way. The person being anxious and tense full stop. Only a resolution of the problem will ease the tension. In this case you do need to have a look at the whole hand to see what has brought it all about.

It is possible, but not easy, to determine whether a condition of stress or actual illness is coming or going. Things *start* first in the positive hand, then move over to the subjective hand, and when both hands are equally affected then the condition has reached its peak and should then begin to recede first from the positive hand, then from the subjective hand, when the whole condition will vanish from both hands. So if you were to find a condition *only* in the positive (generally the right hand) then you know it is just starting. If only in the subjective hand (generally the left) you know it is on its way out.

THE FINGERPRINT PATTERNS AS HEALTH INDICATORS

As mentioned earlier, these patterns (Figure 17) symbolise our basic characteristics and so form the unchanging part of our character structure. It is easy to understand then that these also influence our health pattern.

The loop pattern

These people have the advantage of being adaptable, versatile and expressive with a tendency to fly rather easily from one extreme to another. Mentally and emotionally they are responsive and can be unreliable, as they can so easily change their reactions. Healthwise this pattern predisposes to nerve trouble, digestive weakness and faulty heart conditions according to the studies undertaken by Noel Jaquin and members of the Society to which he belonged.

The arch pattern

The owners of these prints are rather serious and intense people. They find it difficult to express their inward thoughts or feelings, so suffer from emotional repression and psychosomatic problems. They keep everything to themselves, being both suspicious and secretive. They can use their pattern more constructively if they take up some creative, practical hobby which can assist in the exteriorisation of these feelings and ideas and so maintain good health. Physiologically, there is a predisposition to faulty digestive action.

The whorl pattern

These people are intense, fixed, determined and individualistic with a tendency to unconventionality. The conventions are spurned when it suits the person to ignore them. What they feel they feel very deeply, but they do not discuss their feelings, in all they do they are guarded and careful. They

116

tend to be rather slow in response and are rarely adaptable, they expect you to adapt to them. Healthwise, this pattern predisposes to nervous digestive problems or faulty heart action.

The tented arch pattern
Highly strung and idealistic, they are sensitive and emotional. It is hard for them to control their emotional reactions. They are often impulsive and find their ideals too often disappoint them. Healthwise, they have a predisposition to nervous troubles. They should not have too many problems to solve as they do not have the determination of the whorl pattern.

The composite pattern
Here you have twin loops opposing one another. Mentally these people are open to two different sets of ideas or impressions. Often they suffer from inner conflict and self-doubt. Fortunately, they are practical people and try to resolve their conflicts by practical means. They can be repressive, critical and resentful. Healthwise, the pattern predisposes them to general toxic conditions.

Figure 19

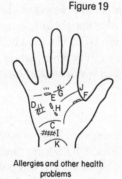

Compound
(Peacock's eye)

(a)

Nail
ridging

(b)

Allergy

Allergies and other health
problems

C . Allergy line
D . Tendency to rheumatic complaints
E . Eye weakness
F . Childhood chest problems / Backache
G . Teeth
H . Islands on Mercury line
I . Gynaecological and urogenital problems
J . Migraine
K . Rascette rising into palm. childbirth
    difficulties. Few children.

The compound pattern
This often manifests as a little whorl within a loop, although any two different patterns linked together in one fingerprint is called a compound (Figure 19a). These are practical people who combine the charm and diplomacy of the loop with say the observation of the whorl, if the pattern is the loop containing the whorl. This is often called a Peacock's Eye, and if

found on the third finger is said to protect you from all manner of dangers and evils. Healthwise, there is a predisposition to digestive weakness, nerve troubles and faulty heart action.

Incidentally, a student writes that he found three subjects with the compound pattern on their thumbs who proved to be dyslexic. Of course this is not enough research to prove anything conclusive, but all research has to start somewhere and this is an interesting point.

In giving these health predispositions it must be remembered that these are merely *predispositions* and do not necessarily have to manifest if the person is someone who looks after their health. There are many health conditions which can be seen fairly easily in the hand if you know where to look and this can help to point you in the right direction as to what is ailing you. It cannot of course give you the whole answer to your problem; that's up to your physician.

HEALTH CONDITIONS

Acidity
This is the basis for a very common chronic complaint, rheumatism, and can be seen first of all in a cluster of little upright lines between the Heart and Head lines on the percussion (Figure 19D). There is a build-up of uric acid, and if not checked then the finger joints or other parts of the body begin to ache. It is wise to cut out those things which are acid-forming from the diet.

Allergies
These come in many shapes and sizes and are due to sensitivity to different foods, drugs or drinks. A very common allergy is hay fever, where the individual is sensitive to pollen. Although the hand cannot point out what particular substance is the offending allergen, it can point out IF you are someone who is at risk in this respect. There is a line which lies at the base of the Luna mount (Figure 19C); technically this is called the Via Lascivia, and if possessing it you were supposed to be a particularly lustful character with a leaning towards all sorts of depravities. Traditional readings change and now it is generally accepted that if you have this line you are sensitive to various substances. This sensitivity can also be seen by vertical ridging on the nails (Figure 19b) and generally you will find that it is substances which you are most accustomed to using and probably enjoy which are causing

these allergic reactions. It is best if you try going without some particular food for a month and see if the ridges begin to grow less pronounced.

Eyes, ears, teeth
Traditionally, an island on the Heart line under the Apollo or third finger (Figure 19E) shows a sight weakness and therefore anyone seeing this in their hand should have a sight check. Very often if the condition is left untreated a series of small lines appears again under the Apollo finger.

An island or chaining of Life line under the Jupiter or forefinger (Figure 19F) suggests that childhood throat problems and bronchial trouble can lead in later life to deafness.

Teeth problems and the need to have a dental appointment can be seen by little lines above the heart line and under the Saturn or middle finger (Figure 19G).

Digestive difficulties
These are generally seen in or around the Mercury line, which traditionally was named the *Liver line*, thus exactly explaining the state of our digestion. If there are digestive difficulties they can be seen in oblique lines coming up from the Life line towards the Mercury finger. Sometimes islands on the Mercury line (Figure 19H) can be the sign of chest problems such as bronchitis and pneumonia. People with these indications should either give up or reduce their smoking level.

Problems related to the reproductive system
This is of course very important to those of you reading this book as many of you will be wanting to have a family. Any problems in this direction are generally to be found at the base of the mount of Luna. There may be lots of little lines criss-crossing and making a sort of veiling there which warns of gynaecological difficulties with women or urogenital problems with men (Figure 19I). I have also noted that where the first Rascette rises up into the palm (Figure 19K) women have difficulty in childbirth, and often there is difficulty with periods where the little finger is bent inwards.

Circulatory problems
Cold hands often point to circulatory problems, that is if they are cold when the temperature actually suggests they should be warm. As children these people may well have suffered with chilblains. Other indications are the colour of the nails which may be blue at the base, very pale in colour,

suggesting anaemia, or red which goes to the other extreme and suggests the possibility of high blood pressure.

The Heart line itself should not be chained; this may be due to some mineral deficiency, or it may be frayed or broken, when a check-up might be advised.

Headaches
These are seen very clearly by little dots on the Head line. If there are rather deep dots proceeding over a length of the Head line you can suspect migraine (Figure 19J). Clinics for this problem are to be found, not in abundance, but in many major cities. Apparently they do have good results if treatment is continued.

Backache
Back problems are to be seen on the Life line in a series of dots like the dots mentioned above as referring to the Head line (Figure 19F). In both cases the length of time these dots are seen on the Head line or the Life line will show the length of time the problem remains. However, if the markings are only on the subjective hand, it implies the difficulties are receding and will soon be gone.

Mineral deficiencies
To maintain good health it seems important: a) to learn to relax and take life philosophically; b) to try and avoid mineral and vitamin deficiencies. These can be seen mainly in white spots on the nails, which generally suggest a lack of calcium and coincide either with the individual having a cold or 'flu.

If the nails are brittle or split easily then biochemic remedies could well be the answer. They can be obtained from any health food store. Where the lines such as the Head or Heart are islanded or chained, then some mineral or vitamin deficiency exists. Often zinc will help the islanded or pitted Head line to think less confusedly and to worry less. Alternative therapists such as homeopaths or radionic practitioners should be able to pinpoint your mineral and vitamin deficiencies and so enable you to make a complete return to good health. In fact, quite often small deficiencies can account for a disabling lack of good health and the enjoyment of life which we all want so much.

For our two friends this has been rather a solemn chapter, but the next will look to happiness and success.

13 Success and Fulfilment

Being able to interpret the message of the hands means that we are able to understand ourselves better and so bring our outer lives into alignment with our inner needs and desires. This is important because although we share a common humanity we are also individuals with widely differing tastes and abilities, talents to be developed, hopes to be fulfilled.

To some the acme of achievement will be the attainment of a degree, to others academic success will mean very little, for their talents lead them in other directions. For some, for instance, the strict training and discipline required for success in the sporting field will all be worthwhile for the person who wishes to excel in the world of sport. The person who dreams of playing at Wimbledon, for instance, who sees themselves as a second Chris Lloyd or Jimmy Connors, will give everything up to attain stardom. Any number of fields can be mentioned to show the diversity of human endeavour and to point out that happiness and success depends upon the individuals aims and goals in life.

CAREER CHOICE

For most of us the correct *career choice* will go a long way towards our sense of happiness and fulfilment. If you remember earlier on we discussed the basic hand shapes and their characteristics in love and friendship. Now we will look at them with reference to career choice. It is possible that after many years in a particular profession, the whole scene becomes stale and the person wants a change. Choice of career then can be as important in the early forties as it was in the late teens or early twenties. Carl Jung, the psychologist and writer, often stated that neurosis grew from over-specialisation in one particular direction. In fact, the man saw himself as Smith the accountant or Jones the bank manager, and other sides of himself were atrophied, and he was unfulfilled. This would be less likely to happen if

Smith or Jones a) did not identify strongly with their particular role; b) did enjoy some hobby which was opposite to, but complemented, their career situation, for instance the desk-bound person with a sailing hobby who is able to get away out to the freedom of the elements on some happy weekends and holidays.

Now let's look at the possibilities for the various hand shapes, remembering that you have no desire to unsettle either yourself or others; so that, if you are happy in your work, there is no need to look for change. It is only if an individual is unhappy in his chosen career, or is restless and wants a change, that one should look to other possibilities for career fulfilment.

The Square hand

This is always a practical and useful hand; the individuals are down-to-earth and like to achieve something worthwhile in their lives. They are good organisers, thorough in their work, systematic and precise in anything they undertake. Above all, they are reliable and persistent.

One might say that it is the Square folk who make the world go round; without them, life would be even more difficult than it is. The fields of endeavour which would fulfil these people are therefore legion, as the qualities which they possess are much in demand. Administrators, accountants, secretaries, engineers, lawyers, doctors, architects, executives, politicians and organisers of all kinds.

One also has to take into account the type of Head line, whatever the hand shape. If the Head line is *imaginative*, that is curves down into Luna, then a job which allows for the artistic, musical, or creative side of this basically practical person would be ideal. Possibly making artistic products would also suit.

If the Head line is *straight*, then this person is more inclined towards a scientific, rational, materialistic career.

If the Head line is *straight* for a little way then *drops down* for the rest of its course, the person is versatile and can veer either one way or the other. Probably, up to the age of about 40 the person will pursue one particular type of career, then change to something very different from then on.

Provided the Square-handed types have a fulfilling career along any of the lines suggested, or of course others of their choice, they'll feel fulfilled and happy. It would be ideal if they had a hobby which entailed some sort of physical flexibility, sport of some kind, such as golf or tennis.

122

The Spatulate hand

These are original types with a flair for action and 'doingness'. They hate to be idle; being loaded with energy and vitality, they like to generate their own schemes and projects, which seem to develop naturally from their imaginative, inventive minds. They excel as entrepreneurs, are often found in the sporting field, and are good in dance, teaching, therapy, counselling. They prefer to work for themselves and often like unusual or out-of-the-way projects. As with the Square hand, the career choices of the owner of the Spatulate hand will be decided partly by the course of the Head line; with a *sloping course* then something more imaginative such as advertising, design, or interior decoration would suit well. If the Head line pursues a more or less *straight course* then a business of some kind is probably the answer – a sports shop might be ideal! For their hobby they would be best with something which rested and relaxed them, such as bridge or meditation.

The Spatulate type will therefore be happy and fulfilled if he has scope to utilise his energies constructively, to learn things, and to face up to challenges; the *hobby* should develop the thoughtful, less restless side of themselves and so bring in more balance and harmony into their lives. This is very necessary as the owner of the Spatulate hand is much subject to stress and finds it really difficult to relax. Probably learning self-hypnosis from a competent hypnotherapist would bring a much more relaxed and happy lifestyle.

The Conic hand

These are emotional, feeling types who are often governed by their emotions. They can make good use of their emotional strength in creative and artistic ways; sensitive and intuitive, they understand people and so make good PRs. They are also excellent organisers, not being too keen on the hard work, but knowing how to use their persuasive talents to get others to do it for them. One thing they hate is routine, so that any nine-to-five job would be soul-destroying for them. They need change and variety and a good modicum of challenge to be present or available in any career. Their forte is their adaptability, their gifts of persuasion, their charm, their eye for the artistic and their talent for languages. They are best working with others and dealing with the public, for they are generally extrovert and confident. If this type of job is open to them they are happy and fulfilled.

As before, the more *sloping* the Head line, the more imaginative the nature and so the more the ability to sympathise and understand others and so to produce literary, artistic or musical offerings which reflect the world in which we live. The *straight* Head line is the more organising type and would do well and be happy in a career of this nature.

The type of hobby could be just chasing the sun or a love of travel and the collection of any number of brochures to sunny climes. However, to develop a more persistent and less changeable response to life they might consider developing an interest in some *one* thing in depth. Anything idealistic or imaginative which takes their fancy will give them a happier and more fulfilling life. A firm hand will be interested in something more intellectual than the fatter type of hand, whose owner will be more drawn to the sensual and material comforts of life.

The Psychic hand

The Psychic is in many ways, like the Conic, interested in artistic and beautiful things, is also sensitive, but lacks the down-to-earth and practical ability of the Conic type, which allows the latter to cope with everyday matters of living successfully in a constantly changing and unpredictable world. If it is just the fingers which are Psychic (pointed) but the palms are of a firmer variety, i.e. Square, Spatulate or Conic, then the Psychic will find fulfilment in some art form, music, writing, drawing, painting, designing, as the owner of the Psychic hand is impressionable, sensitive and creative. They would be happier if they made an effort to approach everyday living with a smattering of common sense, or took to themselves a down-to-earth partner.

The mounts

We have dealt with these earlier and seen how important they are in understanding the character behind the hand. They can also give us additional information on the choices open to a person in trying to achieve happiness and self-fulfilment. So I would suggest to our two friends that they size up the hands in relation to the mounts and see which mounts or mount seems to be the most pronounced.

The Jupiter mount under the forefinger

If this mount appears to be the most pronounced, this person is a leader and would be happy either at the head of a group or running their own concern. This Jupiterian streak might draw them to the Church, the law, politics or to a career working with animals, particularly horses. They might also be drawn into teaching or lecturing.

The Saturn mount under the middle finger

If this mount appears to be the most pronounced, the individual is likely to be a 'loner'. Attracted to deep philosophical or scientific subjects, this is someone who likes their own company. Depending on the skin type, coarse or fine, the call will be to the land, to craft work or to mathematical or medical research. Religion and music of the traditional type also attract the Saturn type.

The Apollo mount under the Apollo or third finger

If this mount appears to be the most developed then we have someone with a happy disposition, who likes and needs to shine, so that a stage career or anyway one which brings the person into contact with the public is just the job. Besides the theatre, the entertainment world in general is suitable, as well as potential for a career in advertising, the media, public relations and any career which allows the individual with a strong Apollo mount to use his/her flair for the artistic. To shine is a necessity for the Apollonian.

The Mercury mount under the Mercury finger

If this mount appears to be the most developed then we have someone who is shrewed, able and good at communication. They get along well with others, are flexible, adaptable and quick to see where their advantage lies. Careers in business, transport, the law, banking, broadcasting, selling, might appeal and bring satisfaction. If the middle phalange is longer than the upper or lower ones, then the law or medicine would be options. Any of the opportunities now offering in Alternative medicine might attract the individualists.

Mars mounts

These are situated at the top of the Venus mount; under the Jupiter finger is the Mars Positive, and above the Luna mount under the Mercury finger is the Mars Negative. Where these are the most prominent mounts, courage, persistence and determination are present, so that an active, challenging career is needed to make for success and happiness, such as athletics, the forces, the police, manual or agricultural work, or a career in building or allied trades.

The Luna mount

Situated at the percussion, under the Mars Negative mount, this is the mount which has to do with the imagination and the instincts of caring, protecting and nurturing. These people often find their fulfilment in looking after their own families or in extending their flair for 'caring' to the professions which extend a helping hand to those in need.

So, while the imaginative side of the mount may well make for the gifted writer, artist, composer, the instinctively protective side would find fulfilment in such careers as social work, health visiting or caring for the young or elderly. As these people generally like travel a career in that field would suit some.

The mount of Venus

This is the base of the thumb and is encircled by the Life line. It cannot be taken as a career indicator by itself, but it does show the amount of energy and warmth which will be devoted to whatever is chosen. With a wide sweep into the hand the warmth, energy and enthusiasm exists and gives an outgoing and kindly nature. Where the mount seems to cling to the thumb, making the area encircled by the Life line narrow, energy and warmth are lacking and this will be noticeable in the personality.

SUCCESS INDICATORS

Now we'll examine other factors which help us towards our goal. One of the prime and basic necessities for success are fingers which are straight and do not lean towards each other, i.e. fingers which are not crooked. Crooked fingers spell a crooked outlook on life and it is doubtful whether in the long run such an outlook and attitude would bring joy and success.

Another basic for success is the possession of a reasonably clear Head line, one without cuts, dots or islands. Clear thinking and good judgement make for sound planning and execution. In fact great potential is seen in the hand where all the major lines are clear and well cut.

Again, in general terms, the hand shows potential for success and happiness if it has more lines rising up than lines which cut across the hand, as the latter represent obstacles.

Remembering how important the Head line is to our success, any line rising upwards from the Head line will be a line of success in some area of our personal academic or intellectual life. A line rising up towards the Jupiter mount (Figure 20a1) will represent exam success, the achievement of a new title perhaps.

A line rising up to the Saturn mount (Figure 20a2) points to success careerwise; promotion, no doubt. If a line rises up to the Apollo mount

(Figure 20a3), then we have a sense of deep satisfaction, of achievement in terms of some artistic, creative success.

If there is a branch running up to the Mercury mount (Figure 20a4), success is likely to come from some business or financial deal.

Figure 20

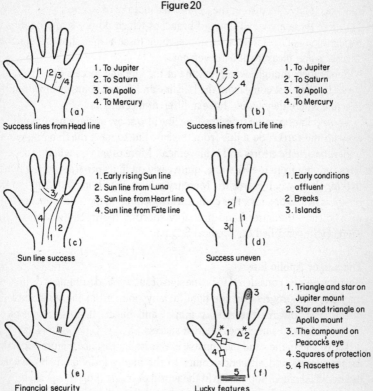

1. To Jupiter
2. To Saturn
3. To Apollo
4. To Mercury

(a) Success lines from Head line

1. To Jupiter
2. To Saturn
3. To Apollo
4. To Mercury

(b) Success lines from Life line

1. Early rising Sun line
2. Sun line from Luna
3. Sun line from Heart line
4. Sun line from Fate line

(c) Sun line success

1. Early conditions affluent
2. Breaks
3. Islands

(d) Success uneven

(e) Financial security

1. Triangle and star on Jupiter mount
2. Star and triangle on Apollo mount
3. The compound on Peacocks eye
4. Squares of protection
5. 4 Rascettes

(f) Lucky features

Success lines also rise from the Life line and represent a time of necessary personal endeavour; if up to the Jupiter mount (Figure 20b1), hard work achieves success in the academic field, if up to the Saturn mount (Figure 20b2) a strong line represents a very important turning point in the person's life, very often the purchase of property or a business and the establishment of a very secure time for the future. This is also true if you can see other smaller rising lines coming up after the big one rising; this shows how successful the effort was.

Success lines rising up to the Apollo mount (Figure 20b3) tell of a time when artistic or literary talent is recognised and rewarded by public approval and suitable financial trappings.

Where the success lines veer over to the Mercury mount (Figure 20b4) under the little finger you'll find the success is in business, commerce or finance, sometimes also in the field of technology or science.

Where there are small upward branches which do not really qualify to aspire to any of the mounts, do not discount these as they show satisfactory successes and pleasure at achievement.

Remember, though, when looking at the Life line success lines, to make sure that they just come from the Life line and do not come from within the Life line where they would have a different meaning.

Success lines coming from the *Fate* line also show achievement mainly to do with the career. So a line from the Fate line to meet the Sun line would underline artistic efforts and achievement. More often you will find success lines running from the Fate line, quite early on in its progress up the hand, making their way towards the Mercury mount, signifying a new job in the business field. For some, this could mean openings in the field of technology or medicine, the latter hand probably sporting the three lines under the Mercury finger called the Medical Stigmata.

The Sun or Apollo line

This is generally considered to be the sign of success and fulfilment de luxe. It may start its progress up the hand at any point from the wrist, but its direction is towards the Apollo mount and finger. It always speaks of contentment and sometimes of great success.

The earlier in the hand the Sun line makes its appearance (Figure 20c1) the earlier success and affluence comes to the happy individual. It suggests public acclaim and popularity in the world of music (pop star perhaps), or entertainment, a singer or dancer who just clicks with the public and whose name becomes a household word.

If the Sun line sweeps up from the Luna mount (Figure 20c2), it again shows the gift of public appeal in the entertainment, literary or political sphere.

While it is fairly unusual to find these early starting points for the Sun line, which if continued strongly would signify a life of success in the public eye, like say the life enjoyed by a prima donna, a prima ballerina, or a top-class musician, it is quite usual to find a Sun line which starts above the Heart line (Figure 20c3). It is possible of course that success in some creative field comes late (after 50), but it generally signifies a time of contentment with what has been achieved in the earlier part of the life and a general satisfaction with things as they are. Since happiness and success are very individual matters and so vary from person to person, naturally it is difficult to say what lies behind the signal of happiness and contentment unless you know the person well.

There will always be reasons shown in the rest of the hand why a Sun line starts when it does. Often you will see it is due to a marriage where a line runs up into the Fate line, or to the help of a partner when the Sun line proceeds from the Fate line (Figure 20c4). It may be the start and progress of a new business which makes the person more independent, which can be seen by a new section of the Fate line starting. Again it could be the ending of a time of worry or uncertainty as shown by the end of an island on the Fate or Head line.

Financial success will usually be implied by the rising Sun line, or the solid satisfaction of a career well founded and built by individual effort as shown by the line from the Life line rising up to Saturn. However, three little lines above the Heart line and under the Apollo finger (Figure 20e) are traditionally said to be the sign of luck with money. No need to worry too much about this side of life is the message here. When you need it the money will be there. A very welcome sign for most of us and I am happy to say it is quite often seen in hands in the general run of a practice.

Adverse markings on the Sun line (Figure 20d) naturally reduce its influence for good fortune at the time they occur. A traditional saying is that an island on the Sun line shows a scandal and this may well be so in that some careless indiscretion leads to problems. Of course where the line breaks and probably resumes again there is some factor in the person's life which is causing the uneven success – possibly a career like that of an actor could cause this, fading in and out of popularity and success as seen in the Sun line.

ARE YOU THE LUCKY ONE?
In other words do you have one or all of these features (Figure 20f) in your hand? Have a good look; you might miss one and that would be a pity.

The star and the triangle are both small, so look well. These are found on the Jupiter and Apollo mounts, and are rated lucky. The star on Jupiter (Figure 20f1) is said to be lucky for any endeavour the subject wishes.

Traditionally, it is said to bring honour, distinction and gratified ambition. The Triangle is good for advancement.

The star on Apollo (Figure 20f2) gives potential for success, even fame, in the artistic, creative field, and is also a definite sign of personal fulfilment and contentment, such as a happy marriage would bring. With the star or triangle on Apollo children are a joy and blessing.

The Peacock's Eye on the tip of the Apollo finger (Figure 20f3) is said to rescue its owner from the most dire disasters so making the person eminently lucky. This has often proved to be the case, particularly in war-time conditions where some lucky guy comes out alive from conditions of apparently almost certain death.

Squares on the hand (Figure 20f4) mark protection and are often found where lines break; the square mends these and extends needful protection to the person at a time of crisis. Again a lucky sign.

Traditionally, a person with four unbroken Rascettes (Figure 20f5) at the base of the palm will be lucky all their lives having good health, riches and happiness. Surely a prescription for success.

It helps then to know the signs of luck and happiness as shown in the hands. Career potential can be pointed out, hobbies suggested, success in the various aspects of life can be shown and ways of improving life can be pointed out, although naturally changes cannot be made without thought and careful planning to bring more happiness and success.

So, my dear friends, I hope you have found this chapter interesting, showing as it tries to do that no hand-reading need ever be negative; we all have at least a few lucky signs and marks of contentment and fulfilment. We all have some potential for success.

14 Gesture as a Source of Information

This chapter may well introduce you, my friends, to a new source of interest and amusement; the more observant you become, the more fun you'll have spotting the unconscious hand movements and gestures. The British are known to be a reserved race, they hate to show emotion, so it is quite common there for devastating news to be met by the recipient with a dead-pan facial expression; but this does not mean that they have lost all feeling, it simply means they have learnt to control and conceal it. Often, however, the hands by their totally unconscious gestures tell a quite different tale.

The typical British reserve is something built into the depths of the island character and is a factor intended to keep the enemy guessing! If you don't know how a person is taking news of an event or situation you are foxed and don't know how to proceed, and strength goes to the silent one, a sort of one-upmanship.

Other races do not on the whole harbour any such inhibitions; their excitement and their feelings are freely expressed facially and in voice as well as with innumerable gestures, which change so often that they can become bewildering. In the end they can just give a general picture of excitability and affirmation or denial in contrast to the more reserved person's subtle gestures.

A meeting and a parting is often sealed with a handshake. Socially we may meet many people in an evening's entertainment, but we will have gained a lot of information from our handshake. There will also have been a preliminary skirmish, an eyeball-to-eyeball quick check-over first; probably more people fall in love at this point than would like to admit to it. Many handshakes will give us a feeling of warmth and interest, will reassure us that we are not meeting haters of the human race. When this feeling of reassuring warmth and welcome is passed on to us in handshake we know we have a normal, reasonably well-adjusted, individual and we may or may not wish to go on from there.

The person who squeezes your hand until you feel the bones are about to be broken is either making sure you know you're dealing with an extrovert or is a really hearty sporty type and willing to underline the fact. The opposite is the 'wet fish' approach, the handshake is hasty and flabby leaving you with an unpleasant feeling of wetness and lack of vitality, which in many cases may be at the root of the matter. The other reason for making such an unpleasant contact may be lack of interest; the person is only interested in himself/herself, even a warm handshake cannot be wasted on matters which do not interest the self.

As you get more used to observing people and their gestures, you will find that the way in which people hold their hands and arms when they walk into a room is most interesting. Some people come towards you buoyantly, expectantly, with their arms and hands hanging free; there is a feeling of 'aliveness' about these people and a harmony in their walk and manner of holding themselves speaking of their continued involvement in living and living creatively. Other people whether they are coming towards you or going away from you give you an impression of defeat by the way their shoulders, arms and hands hang dejectedly and idly in a slumped position. You feel they would also sit like that, all crumpled up and sullen.

Harmony of movement is another thing which is important to note. If you watch some people coming towards you, you will see the nervous person rushing along; if it's a woman on high heels, she'll be going tippedy-tap, her hands distractedly trying to find her ticket in her bag, or straightening her hair, pulling her coat together in a generally nervous and rushed manner. Men who are in a hurry often just rush along, pushing everybody out of the way with their hands or their attaché case, their faces screwed up with anxiety and tension. In these cases, harmony of movement is definitely missing.

Let's consider for a moment how people come over in a social situation and what we can gather from their method of approach. If you like a warm, friendly type who really wants to be liked, you might go for the double handshake. Your hand is grasped by two eager hands, squeezed and gyrated a bit and returned to you as they draw perceptibly close, possibly touch you lightly on the arm or shoulder and generally give out the impression of a friendly spaniel. This person wants to be liked, to be your friend and/or lover, both hopefully at a later date of course.

Another approach comes from the person who offers you two fingers, all the time looking away from you in a simulated, detached, attitude, a sort of 'can't be bothered' message is given out and received by you. A cool fish, loves self first and last, therefore by implication is not interested in meeting you or furthering acquaintance in friendship or love.

Occasionally, a woman can have a pleasant, but perhaps, unless she's geared up to it, embarrassing moment. A man upon being introduced to her can bend low over her hand and raising it carefully to his lips will kiss it tenderly and will then stand back and make a deep bow. This is a more Southern European or South American customary form of greeting than the more informal methods to which we are used. Your reaction to it will depend on how romantic you are. If you are a romantic at heart you will be pleased and touched by this courtly other-worldly gesture. If you're not the romantic type you'll mutter silently, confused and perhaps embarrassed at this out-of-the-ordinary approach.

Then there's the type who has been standing with his hands stuck into the pockets of his jeans; he takes them out and shakes your hand heartily then immediately replaces his hands in his pockets. So he continues to maintain his individuality unimpaired by implying you were just an exercise in duty or good manners.

If at a party you see someone standing with his arms folded across his chest you know you've hit a defensive individual. He does not wish to be involved. Every lecturer or teacher knows they are shut out from the world of the student who sits with his arms crossed. He's probably not listening, but if he is he's not accepting the lesson or lecture. At its best it can be said to be an attitude of caution and wariness and if many of the students at a lecture have this attitude the poor lecturer will have a hard time with little or no interest or encouragement coming from the students. More often the hands go down as interest increases, but it may be hard work at first to make a breakthrough and catch the real interest and involvement of the students. As we are now speaking socially, the implication is that the person who sits or stands with arms crossed over chest does not wish to be involved, he is protecting himself, you'll have a job to get him to let up, he'll probably only answer you in monosyllables and leave the conversation and its direction to you.

Should you see someone sitting down with hands and arms folded across the chest and his legs crossed as well you've got the original defender, not of the Faith, but of himself and his secrets. He is afraid to let go – you might wheedle some of his secrets out! He would then feel naked and unprotected. Fear is at the back of all these funny little habits and inhibitions; fear of others and how they might harm us if we allow them in too close. It's a shame, as much is lost by mistaken attitudes, which shut off people from each other in what could be friendly relationships.

Then there's the chap who gets you into a corner and proceeds to ride his pet hobby horse. Meantime, he shakes his forefinger at you to emphasise his points, you feel completely at his mercy, hemmed into your corner being verbally attacked without much hope of relief until some kind friend, seeing your plight, comes to your rescue. You don't want him doing this over the years do you? He is oblivious to his surroundings, you have become his audience and his forefinger waggles tiresomely in front of your nose. Hopefully you will not be too long a prisoner of such a bore.

Then there's the fidget, the restless type who can never be still; he fidgets with his tie (if he has one), adjusts his collar, scratches his head or his ear. Some people also pick at their fingers, even worse some bite their nails or the skin around the nail. These people are very tense and anxious, also self-destructive as they are, after all, eating themselves. If you point this out to them in a kindly sort of way, they tend to stop and consider as the horrific side of their habit hits them, then usually back they go, obviously to help them digest your words and their own nails. The nail-biters could of course be short of vitamins and minerals, so a vitamin and mineral supplement might not come amiss.

Thumbs represent the vitality and the will to live. In the old days the midwife knew that she could not save the baby whose thumbs were tucked inside the hand; the thumbs had to come out before the first week was out for the baby to live. So look very carefully at the way in which people hold their thumbs when they are sitting in a restful position. If they hold their thumbs outside the hands when at rest, this if fine and absolutely normal; the person is competent and able to cope. Unless you want a lot of demands made upon you be wary of allying yourself with the man who folds his thumbs inside his hands when at rest; he'll like a lot of mothering, and so you might end up finding you've got yourself a child rather than a husband. Of course there are people, usually women, who like to protect others so much that they can extend their mothering instincts from their children to their husbands. Generally these kindly types like to receive a bit of looking after in return, something which the clinging-ivy type of male does not know how to give; therefore such a relationship would be too one-sided to be happy and give fulfilment to both parties.

15 How to take Hand Outlines and Prints

Throughout this book we have considered two people interested in each other, good friends who would like to know a bit more about each other. The suggestion has been that you check your friend's hands quite informally in line with the information given in each chapter so that eventually you are both able to build up quite a comprehensive picture, taking note of the characteristics as they are found and if possible keeping a little notebook of the findings in each case. This is fine as far as it goes, but some of you may like to try your hand at taking either *outlines* of the hand or actual hand prints. The latter of course give more information than the former, but as the hand shape is the basic guide to character the outlines will also be informative.

So for those of you who would like to try your hand at taking outlines and feel that the hand printing could be too difficult and messy, here's how.

HAND OUTLINES

First of all you need a table, a chair and a friend willing to be your 'victim'. Have a little pile of magazines or folded newspapers on your table and on these put one or two sheets of good quality A4 paper. You also need a felt-tipped pen, black for preference. Ask your co-operative friend to shake one hand, making sure he is sitting comfortably and evenly on the chair. The hand which is going to be placed on the paper must be shaken from the wrist until it is absolutely relaxed. Now tell your friend to put his hand palm downwards on the paper and press it down adequately. Do not say *how* it should be put down, the subject must choose how to do this himself. Ask your friend to keep the hand very still once the position has been taken up, so that even when you come around with your pen he should not try and accommodate you by moving his fingers or thumbs when he feels you trotting neatly round the perimeter of his hand. The difference between

135

success and failure can be measured by the absolute stillness of the hands when you are trying to do this operation.

Hold your felt pen upright and keep it upright as you outline the hand; keep as close to the hand as you can without squashing it in. Mark some of the wrist, say half an inch, then holding the paper ask your subject to lift his hand off carefully as if he was peeling it off. If at first you don't succeed, try, try, try again, and you will.

At the top of your paper write in the person's name, date of birth, and the date when you took the outline. If you want other details such as colour of nails, hands, texture of skin and size of mounts these should be noted at the head of the paper, as it adds to the information you can gain from the interpretation of the basic hand shape.

It is often easier in terms of time, mess and expertise to gain a few hand outlines as you start to study hands than it is to go in for full hand prints which are a bit more complex, and if you wanted to do them in style you would need to chase around for your equipment and spend a bit of money to finance your hobby.

HOW TO TAKE A PRINT

You will need the same basics including of course your willing friend and victim. Your table, chair, A4 paper and some water-based lino printing ink – black is the best colour as it makes the hands and the lines stand out well, but it is often difficult to get in black for some reason best known to the trade. The lino printing ink can be obtained at any art shop where you can also usually obtain a 4-in roller; if not you'll be able to pick up one in any photographic shop.

You will also need a square of non-porous material such as glass or perspex on which to put your blob of ink, in order to be able to roll the ink onto your roller and so onto the palm of your hand.

Now, besides using the water-based lino printing ink, you can if you like use finger-printing ink, but I don't advise it as it is extremely messy and hard to get off; its shadow may well remain with your victim for a few days after the operation.

Many amateurs use lipstick which is also messy and hard to get off and does not print well, for after all you are not going to use your best and most expensive lipstick to take prints.

Prior to starting your printing operation you will need to see that you have on your table a small pile of magazines, a few sheets of good quality A4 paper, a pen with which to mark your prints, a 12-in square of glass, formica or perspex, your tube of ink and your 4-in roller.

Again you need to ask your friend to shake his hand, the one he is going to lay down on the paper when you have coated it evenly with the ink. In order to do this operation you need to squeeze a small amount of ink, enough to cover a sixpence, on to your square of glass (formica, perspex); you then roll your roller over this until the roller is evenly covered. You then coat your friend's hand evenly and ask him to place it on the A4 sheet. You now take your felt pen and holding it upright you draw around the whole hand. Remember the subject must remain absolutely still throughout this operation.

Now we come to the crucial bit; when you have done this tell your friend to raise his hand slightly without pulling it off the paper. You then put your right hand over the outside of your friend's hand and with the left hand *push up* gently but firmly against your own hand so that the 'well' which is so often missing in amateur prints comes out. You then peel off the paper and repeat with the other hand. Take one or two prints as you may be very dissatisfied with the early results. There are many possibilities which can lead on to disappointment; for instance, if the subject moves a hair's breadth as you pass by with your pen, or if the subject has high Mounts, then, unless you do the maneouevre I just suggested, you'll have a nasty white void in the centre of your subject's palm print instead of the lovely lines you had hoped to see.

Do see that you have the ink well spread on the roller, for if you have a blotch on one side and nothing on the other this is going to do very little for your imprint. Make sure your subject has relaxed his hands and puts them down on the paper according to his fancy (as this is as you know an important point in interpretation). Do not forget to outline the hands before you ask him to lift them up without the paper falling away from his hands.

Another little point which will be helpful to you in terms of interpretation is that after you have either taken the outline or the print, it does not matter which, you should really take a print or an outline of the thumb as this is such an important pointer to the subject's character, intelligence, will-power and health that you really need a separate picture of it.

To this end, if you are taking an outline, move the paper with the magazines underneath it to the edge of the table, then ask your subject to place his thumb along the edge of the table with the thumb pointing inwards. Now outline the thumb.

If you are taking a print, again move the paper to the edge of the table, then ask your subject to hold up his thumb for you to cover it lightly with a little more water-based lino ink, then ask him to place the thumb at the edge of the table with the thumb pointing inwards – again outline the thumb.

You need to press down the thumb, as you of course also need to press down the hand lightly, although some people like to do their own pressing, but as the object of the exercise is to get good readable prints it is wise to see that all the instructions are followed as closely as possible.

Later you can point your friends to the bathroom and tell them with pride that it will all come off easily with a little soap and water. Meanwhile you need to mark up your print as advised for the outlines and to take your equipment, wash it well and put it away in a little box or bag against the time when you will need to use it all again. Do see that the tube of ink is shut well or the ink will dry up and become difficult to use.

Even if you do not go on to the problems of taking hand prints I hope that you will find interest and information over the chapters of this book and that it will help you to see yourself as others see you. The lines of the hand do not represent immutable destiny; it is we ourselves, who, like spiders who weave their gossamer webs at the dawn of time, weave our own future; and I hope that many of you will find it just that little bit easier to understand your partners and yourselves as a result of information you found in this book.

Good luck and may you find happiness and joy in your lives through partnership and a loving relationship.

Appendix: Reincarnation

A few years ago a member of our Society, Andrew Fitzherbert, told us of his researches into reincarnation and how it might be seen in the hand.

In stating his theory he mentions that if you study many hands you are struck by the many different line patterns. Moreover it is much easier to read events in some hands than in others, with this ability also extending into their future. It is true too that many hands have a multitude of lines yet yield little in terms of events. There are also hands which are completely bare of 'event lines'.

Where a hand-reading gives a correct picture of past happenings and ventures onto the client's future prospects which later prove correct, the suggestion is that this is someone who is living a series of progressive lifetimes. The client has a few 'karmic' debts to be repaid and it is these which are mapped in his hand to be worked out. He mentions that in rare cases he has come across someone with a deeply marked tangle of lines sometimes sporting two or more Life and Head lines. The client has been confused and is finding difficulty in social orientation. Here, the suggestion is that this might be a person who is just starting a series of rebirths and the lines reflect several lifetimes ahead rather than the single lifetime he is trying to live with such difficulty.

He also mentions that perhaps the empty hand, with just the main lines showing, marks the first few lifetimes after the initial start. These people are free to make their own future, but after a few lives their hands will begin to look like the 'many events' type of hand mentioned above.

Then there are the people who are trying to tie up the loose ends from many lives, they are more subject to 'Fate' than others less advanced. Here the hands have many easily-read clear-cut lines relating to the past.

In personality these are bright, intelligent, vital types, and the theory goes that these may be nearing the end of a cycle of rebirths, perhaps at the last incarnation before they pass on to something else.

An interesting fact that Mr Fitzherbert mentions is that it is not widely known that the hands of a newborn baby are often covered with a complex pattern of lines, which fade after birth and are replaced by another set of lines which develop as the child grows. An Indian theory is that the first pattern is in fact that of the last incarnation. It would of course be difficult to research this theory.

Ian Stephenson's researches into reincarnation, some of which cases are mentioned in his book *Twenty Cases Suggestive of Reincarnation*, does mention that investigation of the people, especially children, who remembered past lives did possess scars and birthmarks just as the people they claimed to have been also possessed. It is possible therefore that if physical marks such as scars and birthmarks are carried over, why not the hand, which shows so clearly the personality and likely destiny of its owner?

Andrew Fitzherbert does lament the lack of research to prove these or any other theories, but I'm sure they will be of interest to amateur and professional palmists alike, and perhaps some dedicated palmist will make it his life's work to unravel the relationship between the hand and reincarnation.

Index